where a
Dobdob
meets a
Dikdik

where a
Dobdob
meets a
Dikdik

A WORD LOVER'S GUIDE to the WEIRDEST, WACKIEST, and WONKIEST LEXICAL GEMS

Bill Casselman

Avon, Massachusetts

Published by
Adams Media, a division of F+W Media, Inc.
57 Littlefield Street, Avon, MA 02322. U.S.A.
www.adamsmedia.com

ISBN 10: 1-4405-0636-1
ISBN 13: 978-1-4405-0636-9
eISBN 10: 1-4405-1004-0
eISBN 13: 978-1-4405-1004-5

Printed in the United States of America.

10   9   8   7   6   5   4   3   2   1

Library of Congress Cataloging-in-Publication Data
Casselman, Bill
Where a dobdob meets a dikdik / Bill Casselman.
p. cm.
Includes index.
ISBN-13: 978-1-4405-0636-9
ISBN-10: 1-4405-0636-1
ISBN-13: 978-1-4405-1004-5 (ebk.)
ISBN-10: 1-4405-1004-0 (ebk.)
1. English language—Terms and phrases. 2. Vocabulary. 3. Amercanisms. I. Title.
PE1689.C37 2010
428.1—dc22
2010025708

All images from © Jupiterimages

This book is available at quantity discounts for bulk purchases.
For information, please call 1-800-289-0963.

Dedication

For my dear friend
Suzanne Victoria Barker

Fortes Fortuna iuvat.

"The goddess Fortune helps the brave," wrote the Roman playwright Terence in his play *Phormio*. His implicit meaning? We make our own luck.

Contents

Introduction

My romping word trips and ornate caravans along the spice roads of etymology are here to entertain you, to make you laugh, and to teach you new vocabulary. Our planet has a big mouth and English has the biggest yap, the most cavernous kisser of all. English is the great thief of tongues; it filches new words everywhere. English has no *Académie française* of constipated, chauvinist fussbudgets telling English speakers which words they may use and how they ought to pronounce them. As a consequence of this verbal freedom, English rejoices in a teeming trove of lexical gems borrowed from almost every human speech system on earth. Proudly, English possesses the most capacious word hoard, more individual words than any other language, more than snooty French, more than xenophobic German, more than Russian, Arabic, or Spanish.

Unlike German, English does not take lively neologies such as the word television and dourly turn them into stumblebum Aryan periphrases such as the German *Fernsehapparat*. *Televisione* was good enough for Italian; *la télévision* was sufficient for French, but German? *Nein! Das is nicht Deutsch.* We must have *ein echt Deutsches Wort! Ja-wohl!* Oh, go do your Wurst!

Listen to kids today in Paris refer to *le parking*. Then hear horrified, elderly French purists purse their squinchy little lips and hiss, *"Mais non! Le mot juste, c'est le stationnement!"* Jeepers, by the time you use the proper French term, some *mec* has slipped into your parking space in a dinky Peugeot and stolen it.

But, even though English has a gloriously laissez-faire attitude about acquiring new words from foreign languages, modern English has a fear and suspicion of words that lie outside the margins of everyday speech. This is part of the anti-intellectual prejudice that darkens the brows of North American brainstems and ignorant mouth-breathers, with their moron's motto: don't you dare make me think. This suspicion of new words, a distaste of verbal novelty, is acquired in school from dreary English teachers still in thrall to Hemingwayesque simplicities. You know their chief cliché from your own school days: always use the simple word, class! Never seek out a synonym or exotic foreign term. Thank goodness I had a father who taught the very opposite: always discover the rarest yet still correct word. By doing that, a young student accomplishes two things. You expand your vocabulary and you flummox ordained pedagogical authority, namely, the dull teacher. That second accomplishment is always a delight to the feisty independent student.

Why should you expand your vocabulary? Should we not all speak in glum monosyllables like contestants on reality television programs busily seeing who can load the most bat guano into a banana leaf and then place it on their parole officer's head? Who needs words, really? Should we take our clue about how we speak English from sullen, letterless thugs out on a day pass? Probably not.

Try this reason for increasing one's vocabulary: we think with words. The rest is silence. After one gets beyond the basic, lizard-brain reflexes—eat, defecate, breed, and keep your ass dry from the rain—one might wish to achieve more: learn to read and learn to think. Well, even the most recent brain-scan studies of childhood language acquisition predict that the children with the largest vocabularies do best throughout their schooling. That is scientific fact. The frowsy school yoyos who snort crack in the restroom at recess and have a vocabulary of fifty words may not be the best guides to a life of accomplishment.

The more words we learn as kids, the higher our IQ tests, the higher we score on SATs and other college entrance tests. There is no argument about that. Want to conquer a complex field of study? You will be forced to learn its jargon, the technical words necessary to ply that particular profession or trade. Do you wish to speak only your local dialect? Good for you! But, to paraphrase Holy Writ, in the house of English there are many mansions.

During the long course of a productive life, you may be called upon to learn the speech patterns of your illiterate parents. That is no sin. But, later, when you are called upon to learn SE, Standard English, to enable you to rise to wealth and power in an international corporation, you acquire another version of English. Standard English will also ensure better marks in school and college. Look at our leaders of commerce and politics. They achieved their goals partly through communication skill, through the apt use of language. We must here exempt an upwardly mobile rap record producer with the IQ of a beach pebble and the arsenal of Iraq. Listen to real leaders speak. For the most part, these women and men are models of articulate speech. They think using words. Consequently one of their rules to succeed is: know many words. It ain't rocket science.

The history of words is just plain fun. So please, prove me right, and laugh as you expand your vocabulary.

CHAPTER 1

Names and Nincompoops

We begin this word tour by repudiating so-called word experts who claim the word *orange* has no rhyme in English. So wrong!

Anna Quindlen in her book *How Reading Changed My Life* wrote: "Ignorance is death. A closed mind is a catafalque." The suffocating black velvet of illiteracy, the muffling death shroud of wordlessness, the hulking grunted monosyllabic quilt of brute-like stupidity, all can be yanked off a human back every single time one learns a new word, whether a common term or an obscurity or even one of my two new categories of flatulence! Each new word acquired and used leads to discovery. The rich green leaf of life and thought unfurls through words. Without new words, you are a slug, oozing across the leaf of life and leaving behind nothing but a pathetic slime trail. So don't believe everything you read until you do your research. And don't listen to anyone who tells you there's no rhyme for the word *orange*.

No Rhyme for the Word Orange? Poppycock! Piffle! Twaddle!

Classical Latin *obtundere* gives us in English a verb meriting broader use than it has heretofore received. To obtund is to blunt or to deaden. There are urban myths so stupid as to obtund one's senses upon hearing them repeatedly. But squads of Internet dullards also circulate verbal myths. These tedious falsehoods about words traipse their tiresome way across the Internet, tiptoeing onto one's computer screen clad in deceit's daily robe, namely, the statement of fact. I'm going to bury one such falsehood right now. What angers me most is the air of utter certainty in which this nonsense is couched. Please note that I address this to the letterless yahoos who make this stuff up, not to my readers.

Here's the sentence of piffle I most encounter:

"No word in the English language rhymes with orange, month, silver, or purple."

Oh really, Dr. Johnson?

Well, you are wrong, O expert with the vocabulary of a centipede. You are dead wrong about every word in that sentence claimed to have no rhyme.

Orange rhymes with sporange. British botanists stress the last syllable; Americans stress the first syllable, making it a perfect rhyme for orange. Yes, it is a rare word. Its more common father is sporangium, the little capsule or receptacle that holds spores in certain species of fungi, molds, and ferns.

Also rhyming with orange are related words in botany: hypnosporange, macrosporange, and megasporange.

Let us compose a modest ditty illustrative of this blissful rhyme.

"Oh I gave my love an orange, an orange,
And she gave me a toxic megasporange.
So sorry dear, said she, it's morning you'll wait till
Because the fern spore is likely to be fatal."

Okay, so I'm not Robert Frost. But let us continue.

No Purple or Silver Rhyme? Not!

Internet know-it-alls claim there is no rhyme in English for the word *purple*, eh? Thank you, O compendium of all lexical rhymery!

Let's see now. Just off the top of my admittedly semiliterate head, I can rhyme purple with curple, hirple, and turple. You want rare rhymes? Add my personal favorite, the verb to besperple! Yep, all real words, my little hebetudinous nincompoops.

A curple is a Scottish dialect word for a crupper or a croup, the part of the leather saddle restraint that goes under a horse's tail. It helps prevent the saddle from slipping forward. I hate to add this old barnyard joke, but, after all, I am shameless. After one has defined croup in a stable, one always adds, "But any horse's ass would know that."

To hirple is to walk with a limp or in any halting manner. The verb is still in use in northern England and in Scotland.

To turple was said of animals. It meant to fall down and die, probably a dialectical variant of topple.

To besperple is cited only once in the *Oxford English Dictionary*, in a sixteenth century tale of King Arthur and his knights where the author wrote, "The grounde . . . was all besperpled wyth blode." In other words, loser-knight blood was splattered all over the English daisies.

No rhyme for shiny-faced little silver?

Our gratitude for your word wisdom, O bard of Avon Calling, is inexpressible.

Silver rhymes with dicky dilver and chilver. Dicky dilver is a local British nickname for the periwinkle flower. A chilver is a female lamb, also called ewe-lamb or chilver-lamb.

No Rhyme for Month in English?

Month rhymes with hunth, an official, in-the-dictionary abbreviation, spoken and written, for a hundred thousand. Let us use it in an exemplary sentence: A hunth of morons braying that something is true, when I know it is not, shall never keep me silent.

Month also rhymes with uneath, pronounced "unth." Uneath is archaic English and now rare, but there it is in the work of the great English poet Edmund Spenser "who he was, uneath was to descry." Uneath means difficult, not easy.

Who Makes Up This Spurious Piffle?

The persons who make up these shabby word claims and plaster them on the Internet are ragtag riffraff who slouch oblivious in bars, drunk out of their gourds, and still sucking suds. Their research for statements such as the one we began with today consists of running the alphabet in front of the tail end of the word. So, seeking a rhyme for silver, they will gurgle drunkenly to their sodden tablemates, "Bilver, cilver, dilver, filver, gilver, hilver, and so on."

They would never stoop to open a dictionary. That would "reek of the lamp," as Victorian twits used to say about any statement that smacked of actual learning by the light of a study's lamp or any display of knowledge that hinted the speaker may have applied the discipline of memorization to some facts.

Clueless amateurs, even should they hit on a word of modest rarity that fits their rhyming needs, will be too ignorant to recognize it. For they know nothing of the million-word bounty of English, the language that has the largest number of vocabulary items of any tongue ever spoken on earth.

Ah, weary me! Here there is rhyme, but no reason.

Now you are armed to deal with the next "amazing fact" that rudely pokes its snout onto your computer screen. Any rule about language couched in obdurate certainty is—certainly—always worthy of suspicion.

Here Be Dragons: American Place Names

Some place names of the good old U.S.A. would make the vacationing reader of a road atlas fall face forward into his box of Krispy Kremes, stunned into lethargic mopery by their blandness. Oh no, not another Bear Island? Yes, Bear Island, so named because—be still, my throbbing heart!—a bear was once seen on the island. Wow!

Yet quail not, seekers of the vivid toponym. The cartographical expanses of American mappery are broad indeed and contain place name treasures worth knowing. A toponym is the fancy geographic term for place name, from Greek *topos* "place" + Greek *onoma* "name." The second element is common in words such as acronym, antonym, pseudonym, and synonym.

Why is the chapter titled "Here Be Dragons"? On medieval maps, the cartographer was often faced with large areas that had not been explored. On these blank spaces early mapmakers' convention was to engrave dragons, sea serpents, and other strange creatures from the nightmare bestiary of the medieval imagination. A map from C.E. 1503 called the Lenox Globe has printed over such unknown territory the Latin words *Hic sunt dracones* meaning "here be dragons."

My contention in this brief survey is that some American toponyms are topo-hymns. Here are place names that sing of U.S. history and the unique mindset of pioneers. These places say who the namers were or what obsessed them, or what stood out about the locality, in ways colorful, zesty, and provocative. Such nuggets of our past may lure us to gather these gems and become amateur toponymists.

Don't Be Such Adobe, You Doobie!

Some U.S. map readers are surprised to discover how many Arabic words are lightly hidden in American place names. Is it a plot? No, dear, it's history. But let's look at Arabic words that tiptoed into God's country through the medium of Spanish. Thousands of Arabic words entered Spanish after the Moorish conquest of Spain, an easy takeover hardly worthy of the term *conquest*. Begun with an invasion in C.E. 710, the Arabic rule of Spain ended around C.E. 1250, but not technically until the last Moorish king surrendered to King Ferdinand and Queen Isabella in the very year that Columbus set sail, 1492. Whatever its precise dates, this Moorish occupation of the Iberian Peninsula was 500 years of solid influence, contributing new Arabic-based Spanish place names to Hispanic maps and adding a huge camel saddle of Arabic words to the Spanish word stable; words that later crossed the Atlantic and came to Mexico and Central America with the conquistadores and priests and soldiers of the line who brought this Arabic-spiced Spanish to their new colonies; words that then migrated north to the United States and stayed.

Consider first Adobe Wells, Texas. Sure, we all know adobe is a kind of brick, a simple brick of fine alluvial clay whose oven is the sun and whose substance is straw mixed with sun-dried earth. The warm tawny brown of the yellow playa clay anchors adobe buildings to their desert stands so naturally that well-sited adobe habitations seem upstarts from the very earth they sit upon. What an ancient word *adobe* is! This old stalwart root is 5,000 years old, found in Egyptian hieroglyphics on the walls of Pharaonic tombs. Spanish adopted it directly from Arabic, *al toob* "the brick" pronounced adoub. Arab speakers heard it from North African speakers of Coptic where it was *toeb*, and Coptic took it or shared it with */t.b/*, its Egyptian hieroglyphic transliteration. Nowadays in the southwest you can hear Americans ask about a wall, "That dobie?" Yep.

The earthen hue of the humble adobe brick is responsible for the name of one of the greatest edifices of Moorish architecture too, the Alhambra Palace in Granada. Its Spanish denomination was taken from its Arabic title *al lak'at al hamra*, literally "the castle red" so dubbed from the sun-dried adobe bricks of its outer walls, adobe from the reddish-brown clay of Granada.

Alcatraz

The penal rocks of Alcatraz, glum stones in San Francisco Bay, bear the Arabic name for pelican, given in 1775, and originally named in the plural, *Los Alcatraces*, because so many pelicans perched on those boulders that brood of penitential doom. Some etymologists say Alcatraz is a Spanish version of Arabic *al-gattas* "the diver," a perfect name for a pelican or gannet due to its method of diving to scoop up fish in its bounteous bill and pouch. But that is only one etymology. Today we have many. In Spanish, *el Alcatraz* was also the name for what we call in English the Frigate Bird. In modern Spanish dictionaries *alcatraz* is the gannet. But wait, more Arabic roots are waiting, hiding behind their camels. Another source says the Moorish Arabs called the pelican *al-qadus* "the bucket" because pelicans scooped up fish in their bucket-like pouches. The modern Arabic word for pelican is *saqqa* "water-carrier, water sack."

Another bird name fluffs its goofy wings just offstage of this pelican drama. That is the English word *albatross*. Apparently British sailors could not quite get their Cockney lips around the weird term *alcatraz* and they mangled it into the word *albatross*, thinking it must have some kind of *albus* "white" Latin root because the large sea bird under discussion was, well, whitish. Albatrosses following the wake of ship were first considered good luck. That the albatross became a jinx, a bad omen for a voyage, seems directly attributable to Samuel Taylor Coleridge who used the negative superstition in his mighty poem "The Rime of the Ancient Mariner."

Confused? Don't worry; the line of verbal derivative lineage is seldom straight, for words that flit from human lips to human ears are bound to get tangled in mispronunciation and mishearing. Oh, by the way, once upon a time alcatraz meant another, different bird: the sea eagle.

Al-right Places

Because *al-*, the Arabic word for "the," is common, many Spanish-American place names begin with Al-. Alambique Creek in California is the Spanish word for a liquor still. English has the related, now rare, word *alembic*. Both stem from Arabic *al-anbiq* "distilling apparatus," a rarish instance of a word being borrowed into Arabic from Greek *ambix* "beaker," "cup," or "the cap of a still." Sort of like a retort, an alembic had a bowl-shaped vessel below containing the fermented substance to be distilled, and above it a neck with a cap (the alembic itself) with a spout that conveyed the misty vaporous product to a receiving bowl, perhaps wrapped in ice, in which the product, sometimes alcoholic, was condensed.

Alkalinities

Alkali Lake or Alkali Flats were probably saturated with alkaline salts. The Spanish word is pure Arabic, *al-qali* "soda ash," "potash" < *qala* Arabic verbal root "to bake, to fry." Soda ash was used in the Middle Ages to make soap. If you studied chemistry in school, did you ever wonder why the symbol for potassium in the periodic table of elements is K? The medieval Latin name for alkali or potash was kalium, itself taken from the Arabic *al-qali*. In industrial chemistry, alkaline substances (e.g. sodium carbonate) are often contrasted with acidic ones (hydrochloric acid).

Davy Crockett's Alamo: from Latin not Arabic

Spanish is derived from the rough spoken Latin of Roman soldiers who conquered and settled Hispania, the Iberian Peninsula. Thus most Spanish place names that begin with Al- are in fact of Latin origin, even though they migrated to New Spain in the Americas. Consider the Alamo, historic battle site of Texas, the shrine of Texas liberty, where brave American volunteers including knife fighter Jim Bowie defended the honor of Texas though outnumbered by the bloodthirsty troops of Mexican General Santa Anna. The Alamo took its name from a town in Mexico, Alamo de Parras in the old Mexican state of Nueva Vizcaya.

But the word is widespread in place names of Mexico and the southwest of the U.S.A. In continental Spanish, *alamo* means literally "poplar tree," but in the new world, in New Spain, it almost always refers to the cottonwood, a tree that lined dried-up streambeds and little brooks. The Spanish word derives directly from *alnus*, the Latin word for alder tree. Spanish still has *alno* for black poplar. Botanical Latin has a similarly derived technical term, a specific adjective for certain plants said to have alder-like leaves: *alnifolius, alnifolia, alnifolium.*

"I Hear the Cottonwoods Whispering Low"

Heart-shaped leaves of deepest green helped to anchor the cottonwood in the hearts of many sentimental southwestern pioneers, for the mere sight of this water-loving tree often spelled salvation from mortal thirst for white travelers. The cottonwood is perhaps the most mentioned tree in folksongs of the southwest.

The cottonwood was a clear sign that water was to be found nearby, water being scarce in desert country and its possible location always worth noting. The word pops up on U.S. maps across the southwest. In New Mexico, Los Alamos "the cottonwoods," was selected as a safe, remote location to build and test the atomic bombs that ended the Second World War. Many a stream, a dry creek bed, the scantiest trickle of a rivulet bore the hopeful name of cottonwood. Grizzled prospectors stumbling along a dry wash at a canyon's bottom blessed the sight of the tree. Wanderers along parched gullies and desiccated ravines and sandy arroyos licked their cracked lips, gulping in mounting hope as they spotted a stand of cottonwoods up ahead. Often the Spanish-speaking newcomers who named a watery location Alamo were simply translating an aboriginal place name already given by local native people. For example, plenty of streams were called *T'iis* and *T'iistsoh*, Navaho words for cottonwood.

New Mexico also has Alamogordo "big, fat cottonwood tree." In the name of a suburb of Taos, New Mexico, the diminutive occurs too, as Los Alamitos "the dwarf cottonwood trees." A city in California sports the collective noun from *alamo*, namely Alemeda "grove of cottonwoods." Alameda also meant any grove of shade-giving trees lining a walkway or a path in a park. Alameda, California was actually named for a grove of oak trees. New Mexico has a county named by the adjective form of abundance, Alamosa County, from *alamoso* "abounding in cottonwood trees." Another diminutive form names the New Mexican community of Alamillo "little cottonwood," and the plural of this diminutive once named a stagecoach stop called Los Alamillos, now lost in the sands of time. There is even a place in New Mexico named by using a third diminutive form of alamo, the affectionate diminutive, Alamocita "dear sweet little cottonwood tree." It might sound to us a bit overboard as a name, but not if you saw it when you had not drunk any water for twenty hours.

Long Spanish Names

Spanish is a language that favors orotundity, long rolling names spun out to a pleasing amplitude. Think of the original full name of Los Angeles. Once in sesquipedalian splendor, it bore a moniker honoring the Virgin Mary and was called Nuestra Señora Reina de Los Angeles de la Porciuncula "Our Lady, Queen of the Angels of the Little Portion." Early Spanish explorers had camped beside a river and given that name first to the river, for there they had spent the previous night, August 1, 1769, on a feast day celebrating a shrine of Saint Francis of Assisi named in modesty befitting the saint's humbleness "The Little Portion."

Another lengthy gem of ornate Hispanic nomenclature is a stream in Colorado named El Rio de las Animas Perdidas en Purgatorio "the river of souls lost in Purgatory," today called Las Animas. That Spanish word for soul stems directly from Latin *anima* "soul, spirit." If you are animated, you are spirited, full of soul. If you have too much spirit, there may be animosity. If you are a creature endowed with spirit and movement, you are an animal. Animated drawings seem to move and have a soul of their own.

All the Indo-European words related to Latin *anima* have a basic meaning of "breathe in," as the great etymologist Eric Partridge first suggested. Their very syllables seem to echo an intake and outtake of breath, breathing in: ah-ni- and then breathing out: -ma. The Greek cognate is *atmos* "breath, vapor," and so a globe of air is an atmosphere. The Sanskrit relative word, way off in ancient India, is *atman* "breath, soul" which we may know in the honorific given to Gandhi, Mahatma "great-souled" from *maha* "great" + *atman* "soul." That Sanskrit adjective *maha* is not as foreign as it looks. The root appears in Latin as *magnus* "great, big." Indeed, there is a Latin version of Mahatma, our English adjective *magnanimous*. A magnanimous person has "great spirit" or is "big-souled."

Native American River Names

Let's canoe down a sleek stream or two with native names. Consider an old Indian name for the upper part of the Ohio River, the Allegheny River. It comes from the Delaware language, probably *welhik* "most beautiful" + *heny, hanna* "river." The Allegheny Mountains took their name from the old river. All over the world, river names tend to be the oldest geographic labels bestowed by early humans. Many river names in Europe are so ancient they defy the etymologist. They are not of Indo-European origin and no one can now name the language they represent. The Susquehanna River took its name from the Susquehannock Indians. The Algonquian roots appear to be *susque* "waterfalls, bubbling water, fast-moving water brown with silt" + *hanna* "river, stream" + *ak, agh* Algonquian "men, tribe of people."

The names of many watercourses of noble spate feature the Choctaw word for river *hatchee* and related words such as the Seminole *hachi* "stream, creek, river."

Alabama has the Buttahatchee River, from the Choctaw language in which *butta* means "sumac shrub" + *hatchee* "river." Sumacs indeed disport themselves in most profligate abundance along the Alabaman riverbanks.

Florida's wonderful riverine mouthful, the Caloosahatchee River, honors the local Calusa people.

Also Floridian, from the Choctaw language, is their self-honoring and self-explanatory Choctawhatchee River.

The name of the Weeki Wachee River in Florida is Seminole and means "little river" or "winding river." It is reported, possibly reliably, that comely mermaids flicker flirtatious fins, beckoning lasciviously to passersby from the pellucid billows of local springs.

The diligent searcher after obscure American river names can even find a diminutive of this hatchee word element. Seminole territory of Florida boasts the muddy Fahkahhatchee River from *fahka* "clay" + *hatchee* "creek, river." Nearby is The Fahkahatcheeochee, from the Seminole *fahka* "clay" + *hatchee* "creek, river" + *ochee* "little, small."

Ohatchee Creek in Alabama is located above some other creek, for in the language of the Creek Indians *o* means "upper" and *hatchee* means "creek."

Putting the *Sippi* in Mississippi and the *Michi* in Michigan

Where we could, humans have lived near rivers. Place names in all the world's languages reflect this fluvial adjacency. As we've seen even in our brief look at creek and river names, the aboriginal languages of North America have a practical toponymy; for the most part, their place names mean something locative and descriptively useful. In this section, we'll examine two Algonquian words, *sipiy* "river" and *mitchi* "big," as they appear in some American toponyms.

Algonquian is the largest family of languages native to North America. Before the European invasion, Algonquian languages such as Ojibwa and Cree were spoken in what is now the eastern U.S., the southern half of Canada, and parts of the western U.S.

People speaking Algonquian languages were often the first native peoples that English and French speakers met in North America; consequently a large number of Algonquian words have entered the French and English languages. The British explorers and immigrants often adopted Algonquian words to refer to things they had never seen before. Consequently many of these native words entered English: moose, skunk, chipmunk, raccoon, possum, persimmon, squash, hominy, squaw, papoose, wigwam,

powwow, moccasin, wampum, tomahawk, woodchuck, and tobog-
gan. Some of the most important languages in this family are
Cree, Ojibwa or Chippewa, Blackfoot, and Lenape or Delaware.

Of these, the most famous is Mississippi "big river." Compare
Ojibwa *misi* "big" + *sipi* or *ziipi* "river." The root meaning "big"
has reflexes of minor variance throughout the many individual
languages of the Algonquian group, such as *mici, meici, mitchi,*
and *michi,* hence the state of Michigan named after the lake. Lake
Michigan takes its name from a Chippewan word *meicigama* that
means "big lake," akin to Fox *meikami* "large lake."

The Straits of Mackinac is the narrow waterway that connects
Lake Michigan and Lake Huron, and separates Michigan's lower
from its upper peninsula. The original form of the name was Mich-
ilimakinak, referring to the island and composed of Ojibwe roots
michi "big" + *li* a declarative infix signifying "this is the name of an
island" + *makina* "turtle" + *-k* locative ending meaning "place." It's
an excellent descriptive of a low central hill on Mackinac Island that
roughly resembles a turtle's shell. Mackinac means "turtle place."

Wabash

The river took its name from the general Algonquian color
adjective *wab(p)* meaning "white" adopted in English from French
Ouabache, from the Miami-Illinois dialect *waapaahšiiki* "it shines
white." To some canoeing native centuries ago, the flowing waters
were "shining white." Alternatively its name may have been
bestowed because there were many rabbits (in Cree *wabus*) living
along the river's banks. A lake in Maine seemed to glimmer in the

northern sun and the native people called it Wabacosoos "beautiful little white lake." Wabasso linen sheets were white as a winter hare, for *wabas* is an Ojibwa word for "rabbit."

One of the delightful North American animal names is the true Indian term for the elk, wapiti. In Cree, *wapita!* is exclamatory and means a cry of "It's white!" The phrase refers to the elk's habit of raising its tail as a danger signal and displaying its white-furred rump as it darts elegantly into piney cover. Some Indian money was wampum, short for *wamp-umpeag,* white strings of beads made from polished seashells for decorative, ceremonial, and monetary use. Its roots are from the Narraganset language: *wap/wamp/wampan* "white" + *i* "string" + *-ag,* a plural suffix.

Wapato Lake in Oregon was named for a local food. Wapatoo is the obliging little duck potato, the tuber of *Sagittaria latifolia,* which floats to the surface of ponds and lakes in the Northwest when ripe, where it can be collected by animals and humans.

Arrowhead tubers grow in the muddy guck of shallow streams, marshes, and small lakes where wild geese, ducks, beavers, and muskrats chomp them with gusto. Observing the animals feasting on tubers, native peoples found wapatoo could provide good food even in the winter. Adult aboriginal people used digging sticks to harvest arrowhead tubers, but children jumped into the streams and found tubers by squishing them between toes in the warm muck and yanking them loose. Wapatoo was then boiled or roasted in hot ashes. Wapatoo, a word borrowed from an Algonquian language, means "white food." Compare the Cree word for white mushroom, *wapatowa.* Other common names are: arrowhead, duck potato, *flèche d'eau, tule,* wapata.

Sagitta

Returning briefly to the botanical genus name, *Sagittaria* derives from *sagitta*, Latin for "arrow." Leaves shaped like an arrowhead give this plant its name. The Latin word for arrow hits the target in another familiar word, *Sagittarius*, the sign of the zodiac that is the archer in Latin, referring originally to the constellation. The arrowhead plant family is found chiefly in freshwater streams and swamps in temperate and tropical regions of the northern hemisphere.

The word appears twice in the technical vocabulary of English medicine also, where the sagittal suture of the human skull runs right down the midline of the cranium at the front. It is the solid fusing between the two parietal bones of the skull, supposedly like an arrow, but in fact serrated, because this tooth-like meshing of projections makes for a firmer juncture.

A sagittal is also a longitudinal section, like a virtual slice through an axis, used to state where body parts lie. This section through an axis is called a plane. One is the sagittal plane, a front-to-back plane parallel to the midline of a body, like an arrow passing through the body. Planes are important in the preparation of many modern medical imaging devices.

Oodles of Schnoodles

Have you heard of Schnotties, Labradoodles, Puggles, Yorkipoos, Minpins, Schnoodles, Teacup Malteses, Golden Doodles, and Shipoos? This list of names was found in an advertisement for pets.

What a revolting concatenation of cutesiness and smarmy nomen-clatorial treacle parading under the name of canine hybrid breed names. Why, that list of names, spoken aloud, sounds like a mother cooing toilet-training encouragement to a particularly recalcitrant infant defecator!

SOME NEW REVOLTING DEFINITIONS

- **A Schnoodle is a Schnauzer crossed with a poodle.**
- **A Schnottie is a Schnauzer crossed with a Scottish Terrier.**
- **A Labradoodle is a cross between a Labrador Retriever and a Standard Poodle.**

How could any self-respecting bowwow hold high his muzzle and cherish his doghood while bearing so infantile a name? Hybrid puppies are fine—if such these creatures be—for mutt-dom is indeed a genetic Cuisinart. But, as I gazed through my tortoiseshell lorgnette at that word *schnoodle*, the needle indicator on my barfómeter hit the top. One advertisement touted a schnoodle already microchip-embedded! Another pathetic puppy had been "dedewclawed." I had to investigate that one. It was the semiliterate owner's attempt at the already existing negative adjective *dew-clawed*. Therefore the first prefixed /de-/ is redundant. But then so are the human hybridizers of these hideous *caniculi* (Latin "little dogs"). Dewclaws, for those of you who will be for the first time near puppy paws, are vestigial digits, such as festoon the inner aspect of a dog's foot.

Another Lilliputian doglet, one I considered buying, was listed as "dewormed, first needle, flea-treated, tail docked, tattooed, no-shed, vet-checked, registered and paper-trained." Shucks, we did all that to Aunt Charlotte before we forced her to enter the Convent of the Blind Sisters of the Grand Canyon Rim, but—do you know?—such procedures did not help at all. By the way, I didn't buy that dog. I couldn't. It was not listed in Debrett's.

Sickening cuteness in dog names is a cross between senility and basic disrespect for a tame animal's being. One day when I was twenty-five, after I had witnessed cruelty to an old dog, I said to a friend, Eons ago when the first starving wolf or lupine wild dog crept wretchedly, hesitantly, to the fire of a shaggy caveman, and, after balking many times, finally accepted the first piece of offered burnt meat, at that moment a bargain was struck between wild dog and human. It was as if the dog said, "I surrender my wildness to you, human." And the human said, "I give you my promise, dog, to protect you and be your friend." Any person who violates that distant human promise is filth. Silly names are not cruelty, but they tiptoe close to a contempt that is oblivious to the dignity we owe to the congenial fellow creatures of our earth.

Arf! One can intuit the meanings of the remainder of these new breed names. I will not stoop to define a Shepadoodle or a Shi-poo. Nor shall I step in the latter. In all of dogdom there can be no inaner name than Shi-poo. I can visualize, in what's left of my mind's eye, the quivering, dewlapped, "dedewclawed" dowager who first coined such a wretched label. I can see some poor little ball of a dog lost in her heaving mammary embonpoint barking for air, pleading to be let loose from her imprisoning bosom.

Of course, I don't want to be a dog in the manger about this. It is all very well, I suppose, for the dog snobs to dismiss all these new hybrids as mutts and low curs. But many accepted canine breeds began in lowly circumstance. No matter how we may vilipend their names, denying their cuteness is difficult.

Italy: Proud Origin of a Nation's Name

One April afternoon I was strolling across Michelangelo's superb pavement on the summit of the Capitoline Hill in Rome. The Campidoglio is surely the most beautiful public square in the world. A happy throng of Italian school kids followed their teacher, not too dutifully, across the marbled symmetry of the square. One of the kids suddenly yanked his earbuds off and shouted, *"Forza Italia! Viva Italia!"* A soccer fan, he'd been listening to the World Cup on the radio. Italy's team had just scored. I wondered where the word *Italy* came from. Word nerd? Yep.

All place names have a history. They don't spring full-formed from the forehead of Jupiter. So, pedantic tourist that I am, I leafed through my well-thumbed copy of the *Blue Guide to Rome.* And I found not one word about the origin of the name of the country I was in: Italy. For me, this annoying lacuna tainted one of the most complete guidebooks available. Nor was it in any of the paperback guides I had in my gym bag back in my cheap pensionc in Testaccio, a once shabby but now solidly working-class part of central Rome.

Testaccio Detour

Testaccio has a wonderful market now and many inexpensive places to eat tasty Italian food. Here you will meet ordinary Romans who are pleasant and who will cheerfully talk to tourists, especially if you make an effort to speak Italian.

By the way, *testa* is ancient street Latin for "pot" or "jar." *Testaccio* is Italian for shards (of broken pots). The Italian diminutive ending *-accio* is a pejorative suffix, that is, it makes the noun root smaller and negative. Testaccio is built on a hill that was an ancient garbage midden for broken pots and junk. Hence *testaccio* = "place of shards and broken pots."

Let me give you one more example of this useful Italian suffix. *Posto* means "place," *posto al sole* "a place in the sun, a happy retreat." But with the pejorative suffix, the word takes on a negative import, so that *postaccio* is a common Italian word for a bad place, for example: *prigione è un postaccio* "jail is a bad place."

Testa was also the common Latin word for the human head, much more frequent in everyday Latin speech than *caput*. Roman soldiers took the slangy term for head with them on their postings throughout the Roman Empire. *Testa* is the source of the modern French word for head, *tête*. In English it might translate as "I took a hit on the old jar (head) today."

Okay, *testaccio* detour over. But dawdling through Rome, detour seems a quite proper *modus eundi*, Latin "way of going about," if not a modus vivendi.

Now let's return to the origin of the place name. Later that week in a Roman library, through the kind help of an American friend, I spent a pleasant morning discovering the origin of the place name, *Italia*.

Italia/Italy: Origin of the Name

The English word *Italy* derives from the Latin, then Italian, term for the country: *Italia*. But originally it was spelled *Vitalia*, literally "calf-land," from the Latin *vitulus* "calf." A *vitulus* was a one-year-old calf. This yearling's name came from the same Latin root that gave the Romans their word for age or old age, *vetus*. And that root shows up in the origin of our English word *veteran*. A Roman *veteranus* was a soldier who had seen many campaigns, who had literally grown old in the service of Rome's army. Somewhat later, a veterinary or veterinarian was a slave charged with caring for cows—older cows—from one of the Latin words for milk cows, *veterinae* "cows old enough to give milk" from *vetus* "age."

Hundreds of years before Caesar strode the Forum, the Greeks had borrowed this root for calf, *vitulus*, and made a Greek word for bull. *Tauros* was the usual word. But the Greeks admired heaps of synonyms, and so they used this word to mean bull too. The Greeks had an old letter in their alphabet called digamma to represent a /v/ sound. But digamma fell out of use before Classical Attic Greek, and so a word that probably began in early Greek as **vitalos* "bull" ends up by the time of Plato as *italos*.

The asterisk (*) in front of a word form means that the word is reconstructed. It means scholars have never found the word recorded on stone, on parchment, or on withered papyrus. An asterisked form is a suggested form based on study of the evolution of the languages involved; but it's always a hypothetical construct, not a linguistic fact. Nevertheless it is an educated guess; not the vapid notion of some letterless yoyo who thinks the f-word means "for undue carnal knowledge." It does not.

An obscure Greek historian named Timaios, who wrote in the third century B.C.E., offers an etymology of Italy, as derived from the Latin word *vitulus*. Now, often, we must be wary of ancient theories of word origin. They were frequently polluted by folk etymologies and fanciful notions conceived by writers. But this is one anciently posited etymology that modern scholars think is correct.

For example, educated ancient Romans knew about the *Italia-Vitalia* connection. Virgil, the great epic poet of Augustan Rome, knew it. But when he came to compose his mighty epic of the founding of Rome, *The Aeneid*, Virgil decided it would be more fitting for an epic designed to glorify Rome, if Italy had taken its name from some long-ago hero. Virgil found in a book about Roman cattle breeding by an earlier writer named Varro, the story of Italus.

Can't Find the Origin of a Latin Word? Make It Up!

If an ancient searcher needed a quick origin of a place name and had no clue, he often made up the name of some dubious ancient king. Varro made up Italus, who was a hero to his people, and so they named the kingdom after him. Italus, meet *Italia*! No historically verifiable record whatsoever exists of a king named Italus. But there he is, parading through Virgil's *Aeneid* as the royal bigwig who gave his name to his country.

Real proof, or at least some corroborating evidence that Italy means "calf-land," occurs a little south of Rome. Now, we tend to think of Latin as the only language of ancient Italy. But before the Romans—and even during the early years of Rome's rise— Latin-speaking peoples of Latium shared Italy with folks of many other languages and races. The language Latin took its name from the territory inhabited by its speakers: Latium. Latium was the "flat land" just to the west of present-day Rome. The word *Latium* derived from the adjective *latus*, which means "broad, wide, or flat." Of course, there's a lot of latitude in its meaning.

Encountering the Osci

When the Romans began to expand southward beyond the seven hills of Rome, they encountered a tribe called the Osci living around the Bay of Naples and on the fertile grasslands of Campania, where cattle and calves throve. This tribe spoke an Italic language we call Oscan and they named their country *Viteliu*, which also means "calf-land."

Another form of *vitulus*, a word that meant "little calf," came to be used by ordinary Romans, especially soldiers on their marches through Gaul and Hispania (Spain). This word was *vitellus* (a dialect version of *vitulus* with a few vowel shifts, common in many dialects), and it became in modern French *veau*. An older form in French was *veel*, origin of our English word for calf meat: *veal*. Is that veally, veally interesting? I hope so.

Vellum Means Calfskin

Another English word familiar to students of the humanities derived from *vitellus* is *vellum*, meaning "calfskin parchment" treated so that it can be written or painted upon. Parchment is not a type of paper, but is made of animal skin. The transmission route is long and many-segmented, and looks like this: *vitulus* Latin "calf " > *vitellus* Latin, "little calf " > *vitellinum* Late Latin, literally "belonging to a little calf " hence "calfskin" > *vellin* Old French "calfskin"> *vélin* modern French > *velim* Middle English > *vellum* modern English.

The change of /n/ to /m/ is not unique. Look up the originals of the words *pilgrim* and *venom*.

Fellini! *Il Maestro!*

Modern Italian has a related word, used as the title of one of Federico Fellini's early films, *I Vitelloni*. The movie was about idle older teenagers and twenty-somethings who hung around the streets as unsavoury layabouts. A *vitellone* is a big calf—a teenager who is full grown but still acts like a little child—a twenty-seven-year-old guy who still lives at home, likes having Momma feed him, and has no wish to step forth into the cruel world outside the house of his birth. Hey, doesn't that same syndrome clog family homes in North America even today?

The suffix *-one* in Italian is an augmentative, that is, it makes the root word larger. Most of the Latin-based Romance languages use this augmentative. Consider the Spanish word for man, *hombre*. But *hombron* is a big man, a stud, a tough guy.

Dobdob, Meet Dikdik

Why learn odd words? The acquisition of esoteric vocables limbers up the word tissue in the old noggin, quickens one's verbal recognition quotient, and lets one strut before the glumly monosyllabic herd one's innate and ornate word-pride. Snobbery? *Mais oui!*

Thus I here propose to share my recondite treasures, both wee words and polysyllabic monstrosities of logorrheic sesquipedalianism. The bill of fare—and in a sense, the fare of Bill—shall consist of both small and long words. From the tenebrous realm of obscurity, I now pluck tiny stalwarts to thwart your word power, at the same time that I make it burgeon. O Paradox, what a cheap tart thou art!

- A dobdob is a "punk monk" in a Tibetan lamasery (from Tibetan *Idob Idob*). The bedraggled dobdob is first shown in classes that he is too much the dullard ever to become a learned Buddhist monk. Consequently, he is set to perform the lowliest functions of Tibetan monastic life: cleaning from stables the ordure of yaks, policing the more obstreperous lama candidates, and shooting down the criminal element among unruly Tibetan kite-makers.
- I delight in the reduplicative bliss of the word *dikdik*. A dikdik is a tiny, dainty-hooved African antelope. Have you heard of the antelopes that leap backwards, the postelope and the retrolope?
- A dap-dap is a Philippine coral tree (*Erythrina indica*), the word borrowed into English from one of the great languages of the islands, Tagalog, where its form is *dap-dáp*. Some Erythrina species make happy houseplants.

- Dander consists of minute scales shed from the feathers, hair, or skin of animals. Animal dander is often implicated in allergic response syndromes.
- To daub paint is to slop it on carelessly or quickly.

Now, how shall we employ to our general advantage this mixture of obscure and common words? Simple. Use the words above in an exemplary sentence:

The dandered dobdob daubed dikdik doodoo on Dada's dandy dap-dap.

Should that sentence ever describe exactly what you are seeing, you may be certain that you have ingested upon that hour too profuse a variety of controlled substances.

Other Names to Befuddle the Brain

A garland of delightsome words falls gracefully upon the brow of the learner as we continue our quest for verbal oddments, gems drawn from geology, from extinct Hawaiian bird lore, from synonyms for the word *idiot*, and in general from the obscurer crannies of the word cave.

The Moho

The Moho (noun) is the common abbreviation for the Mohorovičić Discontinuity, named after the extremely well-known Croatian seismologist Andrija Mohorovičić. In 1909 he identified the boundary between the earth's crust and its mantle by discovering during an earthquake an alteration in the speed of quake shockwaves as they traveled across this boundary. The Moho is located about ten kilometers under the bed of oceans and forty-five kilometers under continents.

'O 'O or OO

The oo, pronounced oh-oh, and also written 'o'o, was an extinct Hawaiian bird, a honeyeater of the genus *Moho*. Its lustrous, tufted black plumage condemned this bird to extinction because Hawaiian potentates, weighing in at 400 pounds to the prince, ordered the birds slaughtered to make vast, billowy, ceremonial feather cloaks for the lard-ass lords of the islands. By 1990, all species of the oos were extinct. States one glum authority: "*Moho braccatus*, the Kauai 'o'o, was the last surviving member of the genus."

In the Polynesian language of Hawaii, '*ō* is a noun meaning "object that pierces or penetrates." The reduplication common to Polynesian languages gives another agent noun and a verb form, so that '*o'o* can mean "poker" or "to poke."

The genus name *Moho* is Maori derived from Proto-Polynesian **moso* "the sooty crake," a bird. The Hawaiian cognate *moho* referred to a different bird, the extinct Hawaiian rail, *Porzana sandwichensis*.

Exemplary sentence: The '*o* '*o* scurried across the aa.

As every deft Scrabble player knows, aa (pronounced ah-ah) is one of the two kinds of lava that pours forth from Hawaiian volcanoes. As lavas go, aa is rough and looks like slag with bubble holes. As molten aa cools after being exposed to air, gases formed by the melting magma escape, hissing and emitting blister bubbles that burst on the cooling lava surface to give aa its characteristic scoriaceous aspect.

Ning-nong

A ning-nong is a fool or a stupid person. The word is still alive in New Zealand and Australian slang, but may have originated as a slang term in northern Britain. An 1864 reference says that ning-nang was a worthless horse, perhaps a variant of ning-nag. I like the dismissive nasality of this bisyllabic insult. When spoken aloud, ning-nong has a tintinnabulary silliness that pleases. The sound of the compound summons up the merry little bells that festoon the tips of a fool's cap and traditionally announce the advent of a jester to his audience.

Exemplary sentence: When former President George W. Bush recited his fumbler's catalogue of rightwing Republican inanities, we heard the sing-song of a ning-nong.

Prick-me-dainty

This excellent dismissal of Pecksniffian precisians and wrist-breaking flouncers has lately fallen into desuetude, and we ought to revive it. Prick-me-dainty is a putdown of finicky, overdressed male fashion plates and males claiming extraordinary sensitivity but never demonstrating that claim.

Exemplary sentence: Frederick, the purse-lipped prick-me-dainty, swooned in shock when Roger arrived without his cashmere shawl. The incident provoked an attack of the vapors from which Frederick almost failed to recover.

Merkin

We shall but quote the terse defining by the *Oxford English Dictionary*, *merkin*: "an artificial covering of hair for the female pubic region; a pubic wig for women." Some merkins were made of mouse skin to which fur was glued. The aptly named Captain Grose in *Grose's Classical Dictionary of the Vulgar Tongue* (ed. 3, C.E. 1796) defines a merkin as "counterfeit hair for women's privy parts."

Merkin may derive from the obsolete word *malkin*, which refers to a lower-class woman and derived from a group of affectionate diminutives for the given name Mary that include Marykin and Marykens. Merkins were used hundreds of years ago when women would shave their pubic hair to protect themselves from pubic lice. Prostitutes wore them to hide disease. They are now used in Hollywood while filming nude scenes.

The delights referenced here lead us to a rule: Never avoid the obscure word, for the ocean of English teems with fin-flapping words. Therefore, fishers, cast wide your nets!

CHAPTER 2

Names Get Even Odder

These odd animal names illustrate the naming humor sometimes found among playful zoologists as they set about dubbing the denizens of our earth. Just as we ought to protect the fellow creatures that share our planet, our ark of animals careening through the solar system, so we may pause to enjoy the merry names bestowed on beasts by humankind.

Vampire Squids from Hell and Other Animal Oddities

This chapter contains specimens of grandiloquent zoological naming that cheer the heart of any lover of long words. I am that. Any place in the universe who can name a fishlet *humhumunukunukuapuaa* gets my vote as one awesome planet. Earth has stepped forth with that ichthyological whopper. I explain it thoroughly below and add another totally legitimate and even longer obscure fish name. Be the first on your dock to catch it.

Vampiroteuthis Infernalis

No, I did not make up the creature's name. There does indeed exist a night-black cephalopod, velvet-hooded, caliginous, steeped in sea guile, a winnowy mollusk named Vampyroteuthis infernalis, a small relative of our regular squid, named by an imaginative ichthyologist in 1903 as "Vampire Squid from Hell."

This waggly baggie escapes not by firing obscuring ink into his enemy's water space as more splendid squids do. Instead Vampiroteuthis makes his getaway by ejecting from his many arm tips an adhesive cloud of bioluminescent mucus sprinkled with floating orbs of blue light. So bedazzled and befuddled is his potential devourer by this concealing light show in the water that flithering Vampiroteuthis is able to scoot away into the pelagic briny to a little nook of safety.

The genus name is made up of *vampiro*- "vampire-like" + *teuthis*, the ancient Greek word for the common squid of Mediterranean waters, now called in science *Loligo vulgaris*. *Infernalis*, the specific epithet, is a Late Latin adjective that means "of or pertaining to hell." that is, the inferno, the fiery, never-to-be-smothered barbeque where we and our sins are spitted and turned slowly, kept alight and screaming through all eternity. The Late Latin *infernalis* harks back to earlier Latin *inferus* "situated below, carried under" (*ferre* Latin "to carry, to bear"). *Inferus* had a doublet with an infixed /n/ and that was *infernus* "subterranean, underground, of the lower realms, of Hell, of Hades." Latin had a neuter plural *inferna* "Hell" and *inferni* "the shades of the dead who dwell in Hell." English speakers are much more familiar with the comparative of the adjective *inferus*, namely *inferior*, because it supplied a common English pejorative adjective.

Humuhumunukunukuapuaa

Next to flit past our consideration is a denizen of Pacific waters whose common native name is startling. For my money, it is the best fish name in the world. Bet you a fin! It is the humhumunuku-nukuapuaa (pronounced humu-humu/nuku-nuku/a/pu/A –ah) or the pig-nosed triggerfish, a polychrome beauty that darts among the outer coral reefs of Hawaii. A nifty trivia question: What legiti-mate English word has nine u's?

Like all Polynesian languages, Hawaiian depends heavily on reduplication to make new words. The first Polynesian root in the word is *humu*, meaning "triggerfish" (Proto-Polynesian *sumu*), repeated to make a word *humuhumu*. Here the redupli-cation serves as a diminutive so that humu-humu means "little triggerfish."

Nuku is the Hawaiian word for nose or snout of an animal. Again reduplicating, the repeated root *nuku* acts as a diminutive form would in a Western European language. So *nuku-nuku* means "little nose or snoutlet."

The first *a* in the name is the Hawaiian word for "like" or "simi-lar to" and the last word *pua'a* is the Hawaiian word for a pig. *Pua'a* is an example of onomatopoeia or imitative harmony, an imitation of a softly grunting piggywig, perhaps rooting its snout through leafy debris under some tropical fruit tree.

Therefore, this excellently descriptive word is a semantic chain and humuhumunukunukuapuaa means "little triggerfish with a little nose like a pig."

Hawaiian fishermen joke that the name is longer than the little reef fish itself. The humuhumunukunukuapuaa is the official state fish of Hawaii. Its name has been borrowed by rock bands, restaurants, and is even a song title in the Disney movie *High School Musical 2*, sung by Ashley Tisdale and Lucas Grabeel.

Humuhumunukunukuapuaa is sometimes claimed to be the longest fish name in Hawaiian, but it is not. That high and grandiloquent honor belongs to lauwiliwilinukunuku'oi'oi. This butterfly fish (*Forcipiger longirostris*) has a long nose shaped like a leaf of the wiliwili tree, a species of small flowering tree in the pea family, native to the Hawaiian Islands.

"Hi! My Name is Pig's Ass Sea Worm. What's Yours?"

Chaetopterus pugaporcinus Osborn, 2007 is a benthic sea worm. The second part of the name, the specific epithet here made up of two incorrectly placed Latin roots, means "looks like a pig's buttocks." But this is a very clumsy coinage by a scientist who knew no Latin and less Greek, and paid no attention whatsoever to how best to form new scientific Latin names. One may actually invent a zoological specific epithet that means "looks like a pig's butt," but, properly formed, it would be the excessively tongue-twisting *porcinopugoid.

However, I would never use that first form I invented—it is ugly sounding, clumsy to say, and awkward. I deem a specific epithet from Greek to be apter and more melodious. Just because we are glumly dissecting sea worms in an oceanographic lab, is no reason to abjure humor, delight, or euphony.

Two requisite word parts from Greek would make an adjective that means "pig-assed" have a form something like *gourouni-gluticus. Of course, I have used the modern Greek word for pig, *gourouni,* and the classical Greek word for buttocks, *gloutoi,* because, together, the agglutination of gargly hard /g/ sounds is pleasing. But one could just as well confine the neological building blocks to classical Greek and come up with the term *hyo-pygic "pig-assed," from *hys, hyos* classical Greek "pig" + *pygy* classical Greek "rump, arse."

Aasvogel and Axolotl

The aasvogel is a South African vulture; its Afrikaans name *aasvoël* is made up of South African Dutch *aas* "carrion" + *vogel* "bird."

I always thought it would make an excellent surname for a creepy scientist in a cheap horror movie: "Please, Doktor Aasvogel, when you suck the virgins dry, do **not** make bottom-of-the-milkshake noises."

The axolotl is a little larval salamander that spends its life in mountain lakes of Mexico and the western United States. Its name is pure Aztec. In the language of the Aztecs, Nahuatl, the word is composed of these roots: *atl* Nahuatl "water" + *xolotl* "toy, child's doll." Xolotl was also the name of a trickster figure in Aztec mythology. Here are some other Nahuatl words borrowed into English, chiefly through the medium of Spanish: *tomato, chili, chocolate, coyote,* and *avocado.* The green currant tomato was named by the Aztecs *tomatl.* The chicle in our chewing gum Chiclets™, is Aztec from Nahuatl *tzictli* "stickum, adhesive, chicle." The ocelot was the *ocelotl* to Aztecan hunters. Cacao from Nahuatl *cacahuatl* means "shell" or "rind."

Numbat and Zyzzyva

Sure, you've heard of the wombat, but consider the unheard-of numbat who simply could not afford as effective a PR firm as the wombat. The numbat is a marsupial that eats termites and looks like an anteater with white stripes. The rare numbat is sometimes called the banded anteater. Its name comes from an aboriginal language of Western Australia called Nyungar.

The zyzzyva is a palm-leaf-nibbling weevil of tropical America. Often the last word in dictionaries, its name is onomatopoeic, that is, an imitation of the zzzzz sound the insect makes. A former genus name of leafhoppers, *Zyzza,* is the probable source of the word.

The two largest English dictionaries reject the word. Both the *Oxford English Dictionary* and the *Unabridged Merriam-Webster* deny its existence, poor little weevil. It is difficult to dovetail those denials with the fact that the word *zyzzyva* is listed in *The Random House Dictionary* (2009) and *The American Heritage Dictionary of the English Language,* Fourth Edition (2006).

It must be admitted that the *Unabridged Merriam-Webster* does include a related word: *zyzzogeton* "a genus of leafhoppers."

Is such an exclusion snobbish on the part of the OED? Quite probably. Purrs sniffish British lexicographer: *We're* not going to conclude *our* dictionary with *that* word. Nyah-nyah. You don't think the OED could be that petty, childish, and obstructive in a matter of etymology? You haven't been reading it attentively, pal.

Thus, sucking a sour-lemon boiled sweet, we conclude our onomatology of animal oddities.

Husqvarna: The Most Mispronounced Company Name in the World

This section began in a little restaurant where I sometimes eat breakfast. It arose out of puzzlement by myself and some local companions about how to pronounce the commercial name Husqvarna, a Sweden-founded and now worldwide maker of chainsaws, industrial equipment, home garden equipment, and so on. After listening to one stalwart try "hussi-kuh-varina," I tried to look it up, but even the company's website offers no help in saying one of the most mispronounced brand names in the world. Finally a Swedish gentleman suggested it is properly said as hoos-KVAR-na. It is a compound Swedish noun made up of *hus* + *qvarna*. *Hus* = "house" in Swedish + Old Swedish *qvärn* "mill" = resulting in "millhouse."

Husqvarna is the name of a town in Sweden where the company was founded. The little town took its name from a flourmill beside a local river. As we just noted, the Old Swedish word *qvärn* or *qvarn* means "mill." The modern Swedish reflex is *kvarn*.

HUSQVARNA MINI-PROFILE

Husqvarna is the global leader in outdoor power products for forestry, park maintenance, and lawn and garden care. They also manufacture cutting equipment and diamond tools for the construction and stone industries.

Husqvarna also suggests that the miller himself and his family may have lived in the building that housed the ancient millstone beside the river Humblaruma, hence the name of the house (*husqvarn* "millhouse") quite probably preceded the name of the town. In other words, the mill was built first and so gave its name to the subsequent town that may have grown up around the activities of the flourmill. English once had a similar word, now obsolete, with the order of the roots reversed, namely, *quern-house* "millhouse."

Quern's Cousin *Qvärna*

Qvärn and *kvarn* share a root word with the now rare English word *quern*. A quern was a small set of grinding stones for grain. The upper stone was rotated by hand and rubbed over the grain being ground on the lower stone. Quern also meant a hand-turned peppermill or mustard-grinder.

By about 1000 B.C.E., various civilizations had developed quern mills, principally so that single families could make flour for flatbread cakes, the earliest wheaten bread. A quern mill consisted of a flat circular stone turned in a circular motion over another flat circular stone that crushed grain between its two flat surfaces.

As querns became refined, holes were made in the top stone to introduce the grain or to hold a handle that could be used to turn the stone easily. The Romans enhanced in size the early small hand mills, using donkeys and slaves to provide the power to turn larger and larger grinding stones.

OTHER COUSINS OF QUERN
- **Old English (Anglo-Saxon)** *cwyrn*, *cweorn* "small, hand-operated grain mill"
- **Old Frisian:** *quern*
- **Middle Dutch:** *querne* "handmill" (Modern Dutch *kweern*)
- **Middle Low German:** *querne*
- **Old High German:** *quirna*, *kurn* "millstone, mill"
- **Middle High German:** *kürne*, *kürn*, *kurn*
- **Old Icelandic:** *kvern* handmill (Modern Icelandic *kvörn*)
- **Old Swedish:** *qvärn*, *qvarn* mill (Swedish *kvarn*)
- **Danish:** *kværn*
- **Gothic:** *-qairnus* mill (in *asiluqairnus* "donkey mill")
- **Russian:** *zernov* "millstone"
- **Polish:** *zarna* "millstone"
- **Lithuanian:** *girnos* "millstone"
- **Sanskrit:** *graven* "pressing stone"

Etymology of Qvarna and Quern

There are three possible ancient roots of the English word *quern*. The ultimate origin of these quern-words may be akin to the root in our English word *corn*, an Indo-European root that produces cognates such as Old High German and Old Norse *korn* "grain," Gothic *kaurn*, Latin *granum*, origin of our English word *grain*, Greek *geras* "old age," Sanskrit *jirna* "worn out, frail, old." The prime meaning of the Indo-European (IE) root is "ripening."

North Americans must remember that corn meaning "maize" is a very late sense of the word indeed. Corn's first meaning in Old English was the hard seed of any of the cereal grains or any small, hard particle. Older English speaks of "a corn of salt"—the word *corn* is a synonym for a grain. In England the modern term *corn* encompasses all the cereals: wheat, rye, barley, oats, maize, rice, and so on. In rural England, the word *corn* generally refers to wheat. Maize was first termed "Indian corn" and later shortened by Americans to simply corn.

The second, but less likely, Indo-European source of our English word *quern* may be found in the zero grade form of Proto-Indo-European (PIE), *-gur, whose prime meaning was "heavy." *-Gur produced later reflexes such as the Latin *gravis* meaning "heavy" and Greek *baros* "heaviness."

I believe the most likely ancient etymon of our English word *quern* is the one that gave us our word for the minor medical problem, *clavus durus*, that is, a hard corn on the foot, a horny hardening of the epidermis caused by friction or pressure. This doublet of our word *corn* came from Latin *cornu* > Middle French *corne* > Middle English *coorne*. This corn is akin to Old High German and

Old Norse *horn*, Gothic *haurn*, Latin *cornu* "horn," Latin *cerebrum* "brain," and Greek *keras* "horn."

"Outer Space Aliens Invade the USA, Only to Look Up Your Wife's Dress"

Hey, dude, it could have been a tabloid headline. Let's say that America's favorite tabloid story happened again. Over some recent weekend, a man and his wife were abducted by aliens from outer space. It set me thinking about the origin of that word *alien*. Late Sunday night Flo and Ernie-Bob Spenser, the hapless abductees, were returned, still brushing stardust off their toasted Hush Puppies. They live in the charming little village of Born-Again Possum Brain, Alabama. Okay, I made up the name of their hometown. Like this wee story, it is mythic but illustrative.

Before I attend to the etymology of the word *alien* and place into the interstellar record a few musings about being nabbed by giant bumblebees from the planet Mucor, I offer full disclosure of my cheerful pessimism. *New Yorker* writer Louis Menand once wrote about the late American novelist Richard Condon: "Condon was a cynic of the upbeat type . . . his belief that everything is basically shit did not get in the way of his pleasure in making fun of it." No one has summed up better the basis of my philosophy as a word-nut.

First, why would intelligent beings from another galaxy who are—let's guess conservatively—5,000 years ahead of us in technology and in life skills, wish to probe the patootie of an illiterate auto mechanic from Possum Brain, Alabama? Do Flo and Ernie-Bob have something up their sleeves we don't know about? Sorry, that should read: Do they have something up their butts we don't know about? Other than their heads? I would guess not.

The Word Alien Lands in English

The operative word *alien* is a direct borrowing through the medium of French from a Latin adjective *alienus* "pertaining to or belonging to another person or place." An earlier relative was the Latin noun *alius* "someone else, another person," later an adjective. *Alius* is very primitive Latin, very stark, very old. The etyma are *ali* Latin "other place" (there) or "other person" + *-us* common Latin masculine ending of nouns, pronouns, and adjectives. So the blunt semantic weight of *alius* is "*that* person, that *other* person there."

Lurking in *alius* is emotional content that has never left the word in all its long journeyings down through many languages. *Alienus* carries the utterly negative undertone of "dirty, stinking, cheating, rotten, not-one-of-us, foreign piece of crap from somewhere else." If you think time and progress have bleached away from the word one stain of that isolationist, xenophobic taint, then I invite you to review some of the current United States governmental definitions of the terms *resident alien* and *nonresident alien*.

The Older History of the Word Alien

The Proto-Indo-European root of *alien* is hel-yo- *hel-no- "other, not us" and it appears in cognate forms from many Indo-

European languages. Surprisingly, it is the root of the English *else* in elsewhere and someone else. The root is in German *andere* "other" and Sanskrit *arana* and Irish *aile/eile*. Its Greek reflex *allos* "other" gives us many English technical terms including *parallax, allegory, allergy, allosaur, allophone*, and the genetic term *allele*.

But I maintain that the root, in various forms such as *hel-, *al-, and *ala-, is almost a universal negative. Although its Indo-European reflexes mean predominantly "not us," that is, "other," a more ancient basic meaning predates Proto-Indo-European and appears in elemental semantic stance as the common negative in Semitic, for example, *la*, which in Arabic means "no!"

Does Your Alibi Include an Alias? Alien's Verbal Relatives

Alibi has a basic meaning of "in another place" and is a compound of *ali-ubi*, literally in Latin "another-where." If you have a legitimate alibi, you can prove you were in a place other than the crime scene.

If you used an alias to create your alibi, you used another name not your own. Alias is a bit of legal Latin adopted from a time when English law records were written in Latin. Alias was a Latin adverb in a phrase such as *alias denominatus* "otherwise known as or called." Often now it is italicized: Samuel L. Clemens, *alias* Mark Twain. In many modern uses, an alias implies an illegally assumed name, although that assumption is not necessarily correct. If one were going to translate aka "also known as" into Latin, one could do worse than use *alias denominatus*.

The Sooty Boubou and You

In English, most bird names are positive and descriptive. But some common names of birds are gushingly laudatory or bathed in descriptive excesses of retch-inducing sentimentality: the ruby-throated hummingbird, the helmeted honeyeater of Australia, the Philippine fairy-bluebird, the golden-crowned kinglet, the tawny-faced gnat-wren, the chestnut-bellied nuthatch. Well, you get the idea.

Another ploy of the wanton bird-namer is an obscure Latinate adjective prefixed to a common name: the cinereous conebill, the striolated bunting, the beryl-spangled tanager, the rufous-naped brush finch, the plumbeous Sierra finch.

Then come bird names of a semantic hint that is embarrassing, bird names that sound like congenital malformations of one's sexual apparatus, for example: dickcissel. It is so close to sissy dick that it might be a homophobic taunt from a school playground.

How about an authentic bird name such as the Sooty Boubou? Sooty Boubou sounds like something that must be cured by an injection of antibiotics, after being contracted during an unwise moment of carnality in a Nairobi outhouse. As for the etiology of pink-footed puffback and black-headed gonolek, only a Turkish urologist treating camel-herders could say for sure.

We need darker, more analytical names for some birds. And I, William of Cassel, with all due lack of humility, hereby step forth with examples so glittering, so apt, as to silence all opposition.

- What of the early morning bird that will *not* be quiet as one slowly awakens? I propose this wee-winged friend be called the Clacketty-Billed Fucklet. Formed on the analogy of auklet.
- Consider a showoff bird called the Needlessly Crested Vaunt-Hen.
- What about a bird of boring color named the Dowdy-Winged Drab-Twat?
- As a predator, you are sneaking up on one of the lesser species, a recumbent dozing postman, when suddenly your stealth is violated. Birds fly from their cover with noisy squawking and frantic flappings of wings, awakening the drunken postman and preventing your taking the digital photo that might get him reprimanded. I propose this bird be called the Volant Pygalgia. Volant means "flying" and pygalgia is a medical word for "pain in the ass."
- The Brown-Beaked Fartcatcher, a bird of conservative feathering and habit, winters in Washington, D.C. Its flocking habitat is just behind presidents, where it hovers humbly and emits a servile call of "meep-meep," and a weak squeak of lickspittle flattery and cringing agreement.

Well, bird-lubbers, that's Billy's bounty for this chapter. Now I really must fly.

CHAPTER 3

Cap'n Billy's Sea Chest of Nautical Word Nuggets

Avast, ye pewling landlubbers! Give heed now, lassies and lads, or we'll keelhaul you for a fortnight. It's time to hoist "Blue Peter," ye cadaverous, scurvy-lean crew of cutthroats.

Blue Peter is the name of the nautical flag flown at fore topmast-head when a ship is about to sail, signaling all persons bound out to report onboard before anchor is weighed. It's a blue flag with a white rectangle in the center. In this section, Blue Peter waves us onward to a study of ship and boat word origins and other choice nautical etymologies.

From the time I learned to read, agile craft both piratical and puritanical have sailed the blue sea of my imagination. The hollow thump-thump-thump of a peg leg upon a gangplank as a parrot-shouldered buccaneer, razor cutlass slung in belt, rum-soaked and tobacco-stained, lumbered onboard still thrills me. Pirates under sail stir a story need, whether an elegant corsair such as Errol Flynn's Captain Blood, a larcenous, whiskeyed old sea raider such as Long John Silver, or the semi-prissy self-mocking Johnny Depp, whose Captain Jack Sparrow pirate movies are partially ruined by the application of too much Caribbean irony. For me, sea novels were always surer fare than movies. As a child I read Robert Louis Stevenson's *Treasure Island* (1883) and the not-nearly-so-good R. M. Ballantyne's *The Coral Island* (1858) a dozen times each.

Treasure Island whispered mutinous advisements to every rebellious boy who read it, seething in a window chair with fresh-spoken parental orders still rankling his gizzard. Run away to join the circus? No way. A guy on the run from bothersome parents had only one choice: sail off to tropic isles, fringed with pubic palm trees, ringing with the bongo tock! of coconut popped on rocks, warmed with hula hips asway beneath brown grasses. I know one boy reader named Bill who hunkered down right beside Jim Hawkins in the apple barrel on the deck of the *Hispaniola*, overhearing Long John Silver plan his murderous mutiny.

In addition to being a ripping good yarn, *Treasure Island* introduced me to some of my first sea words, beginning a lifelong liking. Stevenson had spent his childhood among sailors and had crossed the Atlantic before he wrote the novel, so his marine vocabulary was extensive. I'm afraid that even in early high school one of my pastimes during cafeteria lunch break was making up pirate names with several other embryonic etymologists. After many cheap attempts such as Long John Drawers had been enunciated, I do remember one coinage of mine that I still consider rather good. He was a pirate captain troubled with colonic polyps and he terrified all ships on law-abiding oceans under the name of Black Tarry Stewles. You see, a tar was a nickname for a sailor and—oh, forget it.

In this section I include sea words so fascinating that you will rise on tiptoe after reading them and cry out, "Shiver me timbers!" and yet you will feel no embarrassment whatsoever. So, come aboard now, ye lily-livered drylanders who know not the sea. But be warned, she be a rough voyage, arrrrr, mateys.

Ship vs. Boat

On most tongues, in most languages, there is robust poetry and salty tang to the words that describe boats and ships. Just say these words aloud: argosy, barge, caravel, chasse-marée, felucca, flotilla, galleyfoist, gondola, brigantine, hoy, lerret, three-masted schooner, shallop, wherry, and windjammer. What a brash declaration: windjammer! "Ahoy, the wheel! Helmsman, ride her down the wind!"

Don't know some of these gems? We explain all belowdecks, me hearties. The nautical name may be exotic and poetic, as when British poet John Masefield refers to "quinquereme of Nineveh from distant Ophir / Rowing home to haven in sunny Palestine." Although Masefield sought only word magic by using that rare Roman ship word, still the quinquereme was a seaworthy vessel. Its literal meaning is *quinque* Latin "five" + *remus* Latin "oar." The quinquereme was a Roman galley manned by rowers in groups of five. Some writers have suggested that the slave oarsmen were arranged on five decks, but five banks of oars would not be a very yare vessel. She'd be subject to tipping, unstable as Nero, on her beam ends maiden voyage out. Biremes and triremes (two and three groups of oarsmen) were more common in the Roman navy.

Other writers of more prosaic bent than Masefield have plucked from a vast Sargasso Sea the names of kelp-slick ships and sweet-hulled boats. We are going to examine boat and ship names, some that you are unlikely to know, but will be glad to learn. So wishes the always hopeful writer of expository prose.

Ship

One of the distant obbligati of public school days, a duty subordinate but essential like an obbligato in music, a duty for which I am forever grateful, was the recitation of memorized poetry in front of the class. Such "memory work" drilled into my word heart so many of the undulant tunes and dulcifluent rhythms of an English sentence that those melodic runs and sweet trills of syllable bliss have never left me. The education system that does not make students learning their language memorize some of its poetry and stand up and recite it aloud to a class is deficient. Reciting poetry exercises your memory and your vocabulary, eases your fear of public speaking, and welds to your very nerves the symphonic word score that is your native language.

When I focus on the word "ship," what sounds immediately and pleasingly in my ears is that mighty organ chord of nautical metaphor and glowing patriotism from Henry Wadsworth Longfellow's poem that I memorized some sixty years ago and have never forgotten:

Thou, too, sail on, O Ship of State!
Sail on, O Union, strong and great!
Humanity with all its fears,
With all the hopes of future years,
Is hanging breathless on thy fate!
We know what Master laid thy keel,
What Workmen wrought thy ribs of steel,
Who made each mast, and sail, and rope,
What anvils rang, what hammers beat,
In what a forge and what a heat
Were shaped the anchors of thy hope!

Ship's verbal ancestry lies within the common Teutonic word stock. In Old English, *scip* was a strong neuter noun. It makes an early appearance in an English text, C.E. 888, in King Alfred's translation from Latin of Boethius's *De Consolatione Philosophiae* "*haefde he sume hundred scipa*" meaning "he had about a hundred ships." In Old English, nouns had grammatical gender. Gender-wise, ship has been a bit of a cross-dresser. "Captain! Captain! There's naughtiness aboard, sir." The word began as neuter, and then was masculine during the sixteenth and seventeenth centuries. Perhaps, suggests the Oxford English Dictionary, descriptive male words such as the ship terms Dutchman, merchantman, and man-of-war made ship a masculine noun, for example from the mid-seventeenth century: "As a ship which . . . cannot move beyond the length of his cable." Yet earlier in 1611, in *A Winter's Tale*, Shakespeare wrote of "The Shippe boaring the Moone with her maine." So, in older English, a ship could be feminine.

But About a Boat—Now, That's Different

A sailor will generally chastise persons ashore who call large vessels "boats." What, then, is the difference between a boat and a ship? Who better to ask than the United States Navy? According to the Naval Education and Training Bulletin 14325, page AI-2, a boat is "a small craft capable of being carried aboard a ship." A few pages later the same bulletin states, "the term *boat* refers to a non-commissioned waterborne vessel that is not designated as a service craft." But even grizzled old Navy seadogs seem to agree with the most familiar answer to that question in English: a boat is a vessel that can be hauled aboard a ship and therefore a ship is the larger vessel. A boat fits onto a ship, but a ship cannot fit on a boat. Some people proclaim the length of vessel determines what is a boat and what is a ship, but this is not universal. And, in general current English, non-sailors call everything a boat. True seamen think such persons ought to be set adrift, feet in water, and paddled down slow-running streams stocked with piranhas.

The *Oxford English Dictionary* definition is worth quoting, for it is an apt summary of many other dictionary attempts. A boat is "a small open vessel in which to traverse the surface of water, usually propelled by oars, though sometimes by a sail."

Frigates, destroyers, aircraft carriers, cruise ships, ocean liners, brigantines, galleons, three-masted schooners: these are all proud ships. Kayaks, umiaks, catamarans, rowboats, riverboats, paddle steamers, dinghies, outrigger canoes, pontoons, and gigs: these are all feisty boats. Submarines are boats too, because early submarines were hoisted onboard ships and taken to deep water for launching. A book salt (a sailor who reads) or an old Navy man who knows his watercraft will tell you that a turning at sea tells the difference. A ship rolls outboard in a turn; a boat rolls inboard. The center of gravity on a boat is below the freeboard. A boat leans into a curve when turning; a ship leans out.

Etymology of Boat

Old English *bat* is as far back as etymologists can currently sail in search of this root. It appears the Vikings actually borrowed the Old English word as *beit*. Often with older nautical terms, it is English that filched a sea word or two from Old Norse. Also surprising, the German *das Boot* was borrowed from English, instead of the other way around. French *bateau* might be related. Iffiness predominates in this word study and shall continue to do so until an older, likely stem is found floating in the sea of citation.

The word *boat* lurks unseen in the highly contracted form bo'sun and bosun (for boatswain "boatman") and in an English surname based on bosun, Boeson. It is recorded in Old English in the *Domesday Book* of c.e. 1086 as a personal name as well, in the Anglo-Saxon form *batswegen*, one which displays clearly its Old Norse ancestry, for this is yet another early borrowing from the Vikings who brought *bat-sveinn* "boat boy, boat attendant" to the Old English word hoard. As to how early the compound boatswain underwent its severe contraction to bosun, well, that short spelling shows up in Shakespeare's *The Tempest* written in C.E. 1611. Only a few English surnames are based on our word: Boater, Boatwright, Bottman, Boatte, and the Norman surname Le Botere.

The Vikings

Because we have had much to say about Viking words entering English, it is perhaps worthwhile to sit down together upon a shale beach, gather around a small fire, offer a plump gull to Odin, chieftain of the ice gods and, under his mighty Nordic auspices, convey some boaty trivia, while stating a date or two about these northern raiders of the English coasts and interiors. If you have not studied their contribution, you may be unaware of how capacious a bestowal of vocabulary the Vikings made upon the English tongue. A good number of the 500 most-used words in English are Viking. Here, therefore, is a list of direct verbal immigration from Old Norse, the language spoken by the Vikings: are, awe, axle, bag, birth, both, call, die, egg, game, gift, gun, knife, Monday, Tuesday, raft, saga, scrap, skate, steak, take, them, they, ugly, and want. That's but a mere skiff of the Viking blizzard that snowed upon Anglo-Saxon from across a cold sea.

Many of these major words entered English in the ninth and tenth centuries. Viking raids against the British Isles began around C.E. 793. As recorded in the *Anglo-Saxon Chronicle*, these ferocious northmen first attacked a tiny, defenseless, but important monastery on Lindisfarne, a tidal island off the northern coast of the county of Northumberland. The *Anglo-Saxon Chronicle* was a history of England written at the express orders of King Alfred the Great, begun about one hundred years after the Lindisfarne raid, about C.E. 890. Scribes continued keeping the historical record until the mid-twelfth century. Because it is a point of high change of our wordstock, it is worth reading how the ancient and modestly anonymous scribes recorded it:

"A.D. 793. This year came dreadful forewarnings over the land of the Northumbrians, terrifying the people most woefully: these were immense sheets of light rushing through the air, and whirlwinds, and fiery dragons flying across the firmament. These tremendous tokens were soon followed by a great famine: and not long after, on the sixth day before the ides of January in the same year, the harrowing inroads of heathen men made lamentable havoc in the church of God in Holy-island (Lindisfarne), by rapine and slaughter."

By the time of the Norman conquest of England in C.E. 1066, when the Norwegians lost their final battle with the English, the last Viking broadswords had waved in British air and prayers to Odin faded forever from marauding lips.

Lindisfarne, O Shapely Word

While this mellifluous island name is not precisely related to boats, one does require a boat to come ashore upon this pious isle. So let's dip into the name origin of one of the loveliest words in the watery precincts of nautical English. Surely island names belong to sailors everywhere?

No more than a land-hugging hill in the North Sea, Lindisfarne is, to me, one of the most beautiful island names in our language.

So we'll stop a moment to examine its origin. Writing in Latin, a Northumberian monk scholar, known as the Venerable Bede (C.E. 672–735), called the place *insula Lindisfarorum* "island of the Lindisfar peoples" in his most famous study of the church in England whose Latin title, *Historia ecclesiastica gentis Anglorum*, translates as *The Ecclesiastical History of the English People*.

Now Lindis is an old name for part of what would become the northern part of Lincolnshire. But I am convinced by another root that recalls the most noteworthy geographical feature of the place, namely that Lindisfarne is a tidal isle, cut off from the mainland only at high tides but reachable across shallow pools on the rocks at lower tides. The Old Celtic word for "rock pool" or "pool" was *linn*. It's a Celtic root widespread among place names of the British Isles. Consider the Irish city of Dublin, its name compounded of *dubh* "black"+ *linn* "pool," in reference to the dark waters of the River Liffey as it flows through Dublin. Remember the opening words of James Joyce's metanovel, *Finnegans Wake*: "riverrun, past Eve and Adam's, from swerve of shore to bend of bay, brings us by a commodius vicus of recirculation back to Howth Castle and Environs."

The old Celtic word *farran* means "land." It is possible that Lindisfarne is a pre-Viking name for this isle settled at one time by visitors from north Lincolnshire. But nearby are the twenty-eight teeny-weeny Farne Islands, and their name we know stems from the Old English word *fearn* "fern." Mayhap many ferny glades abounded when men first stepped ashore.

Lindisfarne is chiefly famous for one product from the scriptorium of the island's monastery: the lush, splendid, illuminated manuscript called the *Lindisfarne Gospels*, now in the British Library in London.

Today, if you would visit the little island, you must look on the map for Holy Island, its present name, a translation of a Latin name, *Insula Sacra*, first given it by the Normans. A visit to Lindisfarne by boat is the only way to go.

Y'ought to Yacht a Lot

The word *yacht* sailed its sleek self into the English language early in the sixteenth century. Yacht's first printed appearance occurs in the account of a voyage made in C.E. 1557, but contained in that great compendium of 1589, *Hakluyt's Voyages*, or, to render its juicy, palaverous title in part, *The Principall Navigations, Voiages, and Discoveries of the English Nation: Made by Sea or Over Land to the Most Remote and Farthest Distant Quarters of the Earth at Any Time within the Compasse of These 1500 Years: Divided into Three Several Parts According to the Positions of the Regions Whereunto They Were Directed; the First Containing the Personall Travels of the English unto Indœa, Syria, Arabia . . . the Second, Comprehending the Worthy Discoveries of the English Towards the North and Northeast by Sea, as of Lapland . . . the Third and Last, Including the English Valiant Attempts in Searching Almost all the Corners of the Vaste and New World of America . . . Whereunto is Added the Last Most Renowned English Navigation Round About the Whole Globe of the Earth.*

Now that's what I call a title. How sad that a recent modern book must bear as a title the glum snort *Salt*. A lengthy title keeps the browser reading; it luxuriates in the word-dense weave of its own rolling prolixity. I've always believed that vocabulary resources are there to be plundered. As pirates once stove in gold-laden galleons, so word lovers ought to raid the riches, the verbal baubles, the rare lexemic spices that a happy fate has strewn upon the heaving hoard of the English word pie.

Richard Hakluyt's accounts of ancient voyages, most of them written by persons who actually sailed on said voyages, are brimming seashells of nautical English. I recommend dipping into the multitude of volumes whenever you need your word sense brought back to life, after too much time spent among modern American monosyllables, English shrunk to a shabby dearth by too many Hemingway-infatuated school marms.

In fact, Hakluyt's collection of American ship logs and diaries and accounts is one of our chief sources of the early changes wrought upon English in the New World. First published in 1582, it is titled *Divers Voyages Touching the Discoverie of America and the Ilands Adjacent unto the Same, Made First of All by Our Englishmen and Afterwards by the Frenchmen and Britons: With Two Mappes Annexed Hereunto.* Hakluyt supported and encouraged the settlement of North America in many of his works.

Yacht came from early modern Dutch *jaghte* (modern Dutch *jacht*), which was a shortened form of *jaghtschip* "ship for chasing." The Dutch Navy first used yachts to pursue buccaneers and sea scum who infested the shallow seas of the Low Countries. But, pirates, being no dummies, soon bought a few yachts themselves and gave the Hollanders a run for their money, so to speak. Yachts were unique vessels, and so the word was borrowed into most European languages: modern Swedish *jakt*, Spanish *yate*, Russian *yakta*.

We know the moment that the word became widely used in English, too. A fast-sailing ship for the pleasurable conveyance of royal personages and wealthy aristocrats, the vessel was suggested for Charles II's return to England from exile, during the restoration of the British monarchy in 1660. Thereafter, the Dutch East India Company from time to time presented a fine yacht to the ruling monarch. Ever since, yachts have been the choice of rich Brits. Consider *The Royal Yacht Britannia*.

DUTCH SEA WORDS IN ENGLISH

Yacht is of Dutch provenance, like many nautical words in English. We shall take a moment to list a few.

- **ahoy** from Dutch *hoi* "hello"
- **avast** from *houd vast* "hold fast"
- **bow** < *boeg* "front of a ship"
- **buoy** < *boei* "shackle, buoy"
- **cruise** < *kruisen* "to sail across, to sail back and forth" > *kruis* "cross"
- **deck** < *dek* "covering," compare German *bedecken* "to cover" and *Dack* "roof"
- **schooner** < *schoener* "kind of boat"
- **scow** < *scouw* "kind of boat"
- **skipper** < *schipper* "captain, shipper"
- **sloop** < *sloep* "kind of boat"

Unbrail That Moonraker, Midshipman

Sail words billow plumply on the pronouncing tongue and keep aloft the adventurous heart. Listen to sail words: moonraker, lateen, flying jib, spinnaker, topgallant, and skysail. And should the ship run with the wind abaft the beam, wave-thrusting across fair weather, then light-canvas kite sails may fly to reap the breeze. And scudding over Neptune's fathoms we may reach port safely and never need to know what lurks in the benthic deeps of ocean or what gelatinous secrets beach waves may spread by night upon the sand for our morning discovery. So, let us sail on.

Moonraker

Rig a small sail so high up, above even the skysail, that it might indeed rake the moon. The verb "to rake" means "to clean." The playful idea is that the sail's canvas would brush against and clean off the darker spots on the moon, as seen over a night sea. It is also called a moonsail or a raffee.

Spinnaker

Racing yachts have spinnakers on right-angled booms at the yacht's side opposite to the mainsail. Fluffed taut to the snapping point while running in the wind, spinnakers are powerful drawing sails that help sailors win races. The origin of the stout name is lost. Folk etymology suggests it is based on an illiterate pronunciation of Sphinx, the name of the first yacht said to have carried the sail. What? An illiterate sailor? One who says "spinx" instead of Sphinx. Ompussible!

One of the most metaphorically delirious and therefore memorable uses of the word *spinnaker* occurs in a well-known passage of critical analysis of the poetic diction of American poet Wallace Stevens, as displayed in his 1937 collection of poems *Owl's Clover*. His fellow American poet Marianne Moore wrote in a review, "But best of all, the bravura. Upon the general marine volume of statement is set a parachute-spinnaker of verbiage which looms out like half a cantaloupe and gives the body of the theme the air of a fabled argosy advancing." However extravagant Miss Moore's clever but prickly praise may be, it is apt. Both Steven's language in the poems and a spinnaker sail filling with wind are bountiful, but may be overblown!

Argosy

An argosy is a merchant ship of vast bulk and laden with rich cargo. But here is a ship word that was indeed named after one specific kind of watercraft. Argosy sounds so Greek. But, in spite of what many earlier dictionaries stated as fact, argosy has no shown connection with the *Argo*, the name of the ship on which Jason and the Argonauts sailed in search of the Golden Fleece. The Argonauts are simply "the sailors of the Argo" from *nautes* Greek "sailor." In American history, the adventurers who went west to the California gold rush in 1849 were termed Argonauts too.

Argosy was first in English *ragusye*, an adaptation of an Italian name for a type of Dalmatian vessel, in Italian *ragusea*, taken from the old Dalmatian name for the port of Dubrovnik, which was Ragusa. But, quite early in English, the word underwent metath esis: the initial /r/ and /a/ changed places. Who knows why? But probably English-speakers merely found argouse (one early form) easier to say than ragusye. Copious Ragusan trade with England cements the etymology. Venetian merchants favored the capacious holds of the mighty vessels. So it is fitting the word appears in the Shakespearean play most steeped in commerce, *The Merchant of Venice*:

> *Argosies with portly sail,*
> *Like Signiors and rich Burgers on the flood*
> *[which] overpeer the petty Traffickers*
> *That curtsy to them, do them reverence,*
> *As they fly by them with their woven wings.*

Lateen

A lateen-rigged sail is one of the oldest known, probably of ancient Arabic design. It's a narrow sail shaped like a triangle and set on a long yard that crosses a boat's mast horizontally. Lateen has been a familiar sail on small Mediterranean boats for thousands of years. It's only useful in calm waters, so it is seen on the Nile River today and also skimming in the littoral waters of the Med in fair weather. The sleek felucca and the plucky dhow are typically lateen-rigged boats. Many an Egyptian tourist steamboating down to Aswan has passed a sleeping felucca early on a Nile morning, with her lateen brailed up awaiting a dawn breeze. Our English word for this sail was borrowed from the French phrase *voile latine* "Latin sail." In that case, *latine* means Mediterranean. Lateen is a goofy English phonetic spelling, so often encountered when the lazy English prefer to guess at a French spelling rather than discover the correct orthography of a newly encountered word.

Canvas

Plain, dowdy canvas may seem a prosaic mate to stand beside these high-flowing sail words, but did you know that the word *canvas* is a derivative of the word *cannabis*? Yes, that's the same hemp plant, *Cannabis sativa*, whose oozing resins produce the wowie in Maui Wowie and other marijuana effects. Cannabis also gifted humanity with our best early sails and sailcloth, and the best natural rope for nautical use. Though largely replaced by synthetic roping, hemp rope is still found on ships, often tarred, the tar acting as a preservative against seawater. Untreated hemp rope used aboard ship is termed white rope.

Etymology: Higher and Higher

So just how did canvas evolve from cannabis? First, you can see and hear how close the words are. Canvas could be a syncopated, slurred reduction of cannabis. Try saying cannabis while holding your tongue. As it happens, the process of derivation was a little more complicated than syncope, and but not much more, and here it is. The ancient Greek word for the hemp plant was kannabis. The Romans borrowed it as cannabis. Then etymologists must suppose a later, unrecorded but plausible Vulgar Latin adjective such as *can-nabaceus or *cannapaceus meaning "made of hemp." From that came Old Norman French canevas, evolving into thirteenth-century Anglo-French canevaz, borrowed into Middle English as canevas, and then canvas.

Cannabis and Hemp: The Same Word

Most European languages borrowed from the cannabis root for their "hemp" word. There are two reflexes, the Germanic and the Greek-Latin. *Hemp* and *kannabis* stem from the same ancient Indo-European word. We'll perform a bit of surgical phonology here to demonstrate.

First, remove the /is/ noun ending from the Greek root, then you have kannab-. The Greek hard /k/ entered Germanic languages as a rough breathing, like the /ch/ in Scottish loch. So now you have *chanab. Latin and Greek /b/ often change to /p/ or /f/. We have a record of two early Germanic forms: the Old English word for hemp, namely, *haenep* (compare modern Dutch *hennep*) and the Old High German word for hemp, *hanef*. Unstressed syllables tend to get shortened, sometimes shortened so much they disappear. That's what happened to the second syllable in *haenep* and *hanef*. They became Old English *hanp and German *hanf*. Now, English is a language that does not like the conso-nant cluster /np/. English tongues find it difficult to pronounce, so they introduce a short vowel between the /n/ sound and the /p/ sound. But there is a way around this enunciatory difficulty. Sim-ply change the /n/ to /m/. English has no problem with that cluster of consonants (imp, shrimp, blimp, pimp). That's how *haenep* became *hanp became *hamp became our modern English form *hemp*.

The Scandinavian languages used the /h/ form to get words such as Swedish *hampa* and Norwegian *hamp*, whereas other languages used the older cannabis as the basis for their hemp word, for example, Italian *canapa* and Russian *konoplya*. Guess what the word for hemp was in the ancient languages of India based on Sanskrit? *Ganja!* From the discovery of burnt seeds in ancient sacrificial fire sites, paleobotanists think that even the ancient Assyrians used hemp. Their word for it was *qunubu*, a possible source of the Greek form *kannab(is)*. *Qunubu* means "way to make smoke." One final question about usage and extended meaning may occur to you. How did the use of the verb to canvass, as to canvass for votes, come out of the canvas used to make sails? Canvas once meant "to toss objects in a large sheet of canvas" and "to debate issues and politics." These new meanings of canvass began to be widely used early in sixteenth-century England.

It should be made clear that the strains of hemp used to make industrial rope do not contain a high percentage of tetrahydro-cannabinol. THC is the major psychoactive chemical found in marijuana strains of the hemp plant. Thus a scene at sea featuring this crisis will never arise: "Captain! Trouble at the stern, sir! Certain deckhands have learned that canvas sails are made of cannabis hemp, and now an unruly element among the midshipmen are grinding up the lower sails and trying to smoke them."

Manila, Abaca, Sisal, and Coir

Natural nautical ropes are also made of manila, abaca, sisal, and coir. Manila is named after the capital city of the Philippine Islands, where it is still made from the fibers of a wild banana tree called the abaca with the appropriate botanical name, *Musa textilis.* The stress in this native name is on the last syllable, ah-buh-KA. Abaca rope is durable, flexible, and impervious to saltwater damage. Thus, it is used as berthing hawsers, slings, falls, ship's lines, tow-ropes, and fishing nets. Sisal is a light rope that floats and is spun from the hard fibers in the leaves of a tropical plant, *Agave sisalana.* Not the same plant but closely related is an agave crop plant of eastern Mexico called henequen, also grown to make rope and twine. Its botanical name is *Agave fourcroydes.* Vast sisal plantations are found in Kenya, Tanganyika, Haiti, and Java.

Coir is rope made from the stiff fibers in the outer husk of the coconut. As you might suspect, coir floats, so although it is not the strongest rope, coir is useful for rescue at sea and for certain salvage operations. Coir is a long-ago British attempt to pronounce the Tamil word for rope, *kayiru.* A single thread of yellow rogue's yarn in one strand of a coir rope identifies it as coir.

Afloat with Flotsam, Jetsam, and Lagan

Flotsam and jetsam in everyday, flippant use can signify any bobbing debris on the surface of the sea. But all three words have a livelier and much trickier specificity related to international admiralty laws and the conventions of marine salvage.

Flotsam

It's easy to remember the difference between flotsam and jetsam. Flotsam is "floatsome," cargo or wreckage found floating on the surface of the ocean or goods seen to float up from the hull of a wrecked ship. Jetsam is goods jettisoned at sea, deliberately thrown overboard to lighten the ship's ballast during inclement weather or marine emergency. In older salvage law, flotsam became the legal property of the salvor, the one who found it. In most current laws of the sea, flotsam is in the first right still the property of the original owner. In the maritime law of most western countries, flotsam must be on the surface, must indeed be bric-à-brac abob on the bounding main.

Parts of shipwrecks found on the bottom of the sea, such as fabled troves of pirate gold or chests of doubloons and pieces of eight, invoke more complex ownership issues. Flotsam does not originate in that made-up form *floatsome. It stems from Anglo-French *floteson*, introduced by the Norman conquerors after C.E. 1066. Modern French is *flottaison*, from a Late Latin accusative singular form *flottationem* from one of the later float verb reflexes *flottare*.

Jetsam

Jetsam, as stated earlier, is goods deliberately thrown overboard. The word is a simple syncopation of jettison, also taken into English during the Norman Conquest and evolving into an Anglo-French form *getteson* > *getaison* > Latin *jactationem* > *jactare* "to throw." The common modern French verb of throwing, *jêter*, has the same source. Jetsam can refer to goods thrown overboard that eventually wash ashore.

Once upon a maritime law, the ownership of goods tossed over the gunwales was lost. You ditched it to save your ship and your life, and whoever found jetsam owned it. The law is no longer so simple. Giant corporate shippers the world over have done their lobbying best to make sure that original owners own everything always. Should some hapless schnook salvage your crappy old vessel, *The S.S. Leaky Hull,* present laws are designed to see that the salvor gets a piddling reward. Were I the skipper of a feisty ship watching a vast cargo ship capsizing in ocean waves, I would not touch the sinking ship or come near it until I had contacted the owners by ship's radio and worked out a legal rescue reward down to the last penny. And I'd triple the so-called "salvage rights" just for starters. If the grasping old Scrooges who own the ship don't want to offer a proper reward, then bye, bye Shippie! Greedy whores! Let them get Davy Jones to salvage their poopy decks.

All that said, a gold coin found on a beach is yours, unless some fascist bureaucrat hears of it and waxes rapacious, coveting what is not his. Hence the common warning whispered by treasure hunters everywhere: if you can manage it, don't tell anyone you've found sunken loot.

Lagan

In maritime law, there is a way to firmly attach ownership to goods cast overboard during emergencies: attach a buoy or buoy rope to the goods, signaling your intention to retrieve jettisoned goods later. Lagan can also be goods lying inside a sunken ship at the bottom of the sea. In many instances the original owner retains possession of lagan. Confusingly, lagan has other, broader meanings: once-shipped goods lying on the bottom of the sea, either loose on the bottom or inside the hull of a ship or still attached to a buoy. The word is an adaptation of an Old French present-participial adjective, *lagand* "lying." Unlike most French words, the medieval Latin term *laganum* derived from the Old French, not vice versa. Lagand may have been a gift of the Vikings or Northmen when they conquered part of France and called it Normandy. There is an Old Norse word *lagn* that means "a net flung over seawater."

Derelict

Vessels and their cargoes are derelict at sea when they have been abandoned "by consent, compulsion, or stress of weather." Britain has an odd proviso that, if a live domestic pet animal or mascot is onboard when the vessel is salvaged, then the original owner may recover the ships and its cargo within a year and a day, after remitting the salvage fees due to the salvor. Arf! Arf!

A British vessel washed ashore is likewise not a legal wreck if a human or animal is alive onboard when the vessel strands. The same proviso applies to a sunken ship. So, presumably, a Chihuahua in full scuba gear could ensure ownership. Glug! Glug!

Ownership

In Britain, flotsam and jetsam salvaged between the low water and high water tide lines can be claimed by the salvor. States the same authority: "On the other hand, lagan and all other cargo and wreckage in the water remain the property of their original owners. Anyone removing those goods must inform the Receiver of Wreck to avoid the accusation of theft." Those laws do not apply in the United States or in Canada.

All four terms vary greatly depending on which nation holds legal sway over the ship and its goods. Both Great Britain and Canada have an official titled Receiver of Wreck to whom all salvages and finding of sunken ships must be reported. In Canada, the salvor does not automatically own what he finds. The original owners hold possession of the ship and its goods. The salvor may be entitled to a reward. Big whoopee!

Wrack

We'll end with an obsolete synonym. I always like a synonym bun with tea, don't you? The word *wrack* for a wrecked ship or its goods cast ashore we borrowed, like quite a few other nautical terms, from Dutch *wrak* "wrecked ship" itself borrowed from Norwegian *rak*. It was a common Teutonic form. Old English has *wraec*. Although wrack was once an operative synonym for flotsam or jetsam or lagan, nowadays, as a compound sea wrack, it usually means seaweed washed ashore, slimy glistering clusters of knotted kelp, wave-cast weeds of ocean depths. Shakespeare uses the word memorably in one of the magnificent speeches in *Richard III* when the Duke of Clarence, before he is conveyed to his doom in the Tower of London, babbles out a recent nightmare:

Lord, Lord! methought what pain it was to drown:
What dreadful noise of water in mine ears!
What sights of ugly death within mine eyes!
Me thought, I saw a thousand fearful wracks;
A thousand men that fishes gnaw'd upon . . .

Arrest Him for Barratry! Or Salty Terms from Maritime Law

As steeped in brine as the names of ships are the names of the legal transgressions maritime folk may commit from time to time in pursuit of making a living from the sea. By no means do we suggest that Popeye the Sailor is a felon. Bloated shipping magnates are much more often caught with their slippery hands in someone else's herring barrel than simple deckhands. The language of maritime law is obscure to most who stay ashore. But, should you be a cottage owner watching a change in lake currents caused by a new factory across the lake slowly washing away the beach front of your property, you may well like to learn about the laws of avulsion and alluvion. This section is our humble attempt to lure you into a new ocean of words upon whose waves you may bob happily for hours, even learning how to sue a neighbor over water rights.

High Seas

The high seas are any seawaters not subject to national jurisdiction. For centuries they bore their old legal Latin name, *mare liberum*, literally "the free sea," term beloved of maritime law-yers, crusty Roman phrase that haunts many a codicil in the yellowed parchment of a nautical contract or, more pleasant for maritime lawyers, a document alleging breach of contract, perhaps a delightful, long-festering default of affreightment fee? When bodies of water transcend international boundaries it is nowadays said that they are transboundary or international waters. This applies to all bodies of water and their drainage basins, to enclosed regional seas, estuaries, rivers, lakes, aqui-fers, and wetlands.

Countries with seacoasts have always tried to assert sovereignty over as much area of bordering sea as they could claim. For cen-turies this was expressed in the West by a late medieval dictum of terrestrial law: *terrae dominium finitur ubi finitus armorum vis*, "the control of a land extends only as far as the force of a country's arms extends." This applied to territorial waters too, and the prac-tical means of calibrating the extent of influence over the littoral zone of a body of water was fascinating. The farthest a fired can-nonball could travel, accepted as three miles, became the agreed-upon range of coastal water claimable by an individual country, hence the well-known "three-mile limit," which national greed has extended so that nowadays a twelve-mile limit is more common to mark territorial waters.

The 1982 United Nations Convention on the Law of the Sea defines the high seas this way: "all parts of the sea that are not included in the exclusive economic zone, in the territorial sea or in the internal waters of a State, or in the archipelagic waters of an archipelagic State." All states now assert jurisdiction over some portion of their coastal waters, often pushing the outside of the watery envelope so they can protect from foreign ships their off-shore fisheries.

Ships on the high seas are, in general, subject to the maritime laws of the nation whose flag they fly. But the universal and ancient doctrine of *mare liberum* or "freedom of the seas" holds that no nation owns the seas and thus no nation may forbid trespass upon the high seas—with one glaring exception, called in admiralty law, *hostis humani generis* Latin "enemy of mankind." It refers to a still-legal "custom of the sea" in regard to the status of pirates, slave-dealers, and, expanded in recent times in a few jurisdictions, torturers. Any nation perceiving these criminal acts against humanity may pursue the perpetrators, try them by court martial of the capturing nation, and, if found guilty, execute them at sea by hanging from the yard-arm of a capturing ship or by other land-based execution.

From many aggrieved quarters come demands that airplane hijackers and terrorists and all torturers also fall under the severe strictures of the legal doctrine of *hostis humani generis*. But so far even the global glut of religious terrorists has not caused them to be legal "enemies of mankind." They are still dealt with under the principle of *aut dedere aud judicare* "either prosecute or extradite."

Alluvion

You own some land that borders a silty river in whose flow much soil is suspended. A change in the currents and flow of this river adds, over the years, acres to your riverside property. One day these acres are claimed by someone else. The reasons of claim do not concern us. To your delight, some particles of this new land contain gold. But the operator of a downriver mine claims the gold belongs to him, not to you. What relief, if any, does the law of alluvion provide on your behalf?

Alluvion is a French legal term derived from the Latin noun form *alluvionem* "a flooding over, a washing up against" from *ad* Latin "to, toward, close to" + *-luvio* "washing"< *luere* Latin "to wash." Alluvion has several connected meanings. It signifies the flow of such deposit-rich waters. It means the suspended matter itself. And alluvion is the process of land building in which the slow accretion of the waterborne material makes new land and creates legal terra firma. The law is, for once, clear. The gold-laden new soil belongs to you. States one legal authority: "That becomes ours which is brought to us by alluvion." You own it. Conversely, should alluvion wear away the sculpted sandy landing at your riverside, can you sue the industrial company upstream who altered the course and flow of the river? Good luck.

Justice MacLean of the United States Supreme Court wrote in a case concerning the Mississippi at New Orleans: "The history of the alluvial formations by the action of the waters of this mighty river is interesting to the public, and still more so to the riparian proprietors. The question is well settled at common law that the person whose land is bounded by a stream of water which changes its course gradually by alluvial formations shall still hold by the same boundary, including the accumulated soil. No other rule can be applied on just principles. Every proprietor whose land is thus bounded is subject to loss by the same means which may add to his territory, and as he is without remedy for his loss in this way, he cannot be held accountable for his gain."

Avulsion is a decrease in land of one proprietor's estate due to a sudden flooding action of water or the violent change of a river's course, and the subsequent increase of land to another proprietor's estate. At law, contrary to the rule respecting alluvion or gradual accretion of soil, avulsed property remains that of the original owner. *Avulsio* is Late Latin "a tearing away" < *avellere* Latin "to pull off, to pluck." Thomas Jefferson liked the rejecting sound of the word and used it to describe America's separation from the burdensome shackles of English rule: "on condition of everlasting avulsion from Great Britain."

Barratry

Barratrous conduct is any illegal act of intention committed by the crew or master of a ship to the disadvantage of the ship's owner, or fraud and theft by other parties not acting in collusion with the crew or master. Hijacking freight is barratry. Gross negligence aboard is barratry. Letting the illegally purchased, illegally shipped, endangered parrots die in their cages because a midshipman made the parrots drink a hypertonic sports drink and the caged parrots expired doing hundreds of rotating reps on their perching bars is barratry. Barratrous conduct might include abandoning a ship's cargo to rot while docked in a foreign port. Deserting a ship is barratrous. Stealing her cargo is most naughty.

The great Blackstone in his *Commentaries on the Laws of England* waxes stern: "If the offender (as is too frequently the case) belongs to the profession of law, a barretor who is thus able as well as willing to do mischief ought also to be disabled from practising for the future." Once upon a crueler time, English law provided that any lawyer convicted of barratry was subject to being "transported for seven years" (sent to a colony such as Australia).

When the ship's owner or crew is innocent of barratrous acts, the liabilities of barratry are born by the shipper or consignee of goods who customarily takes out marine insurance against barratry.

Barratry is a loan word brought to England by the Norman French. In Old French it was *baraterie* from *barat* "deceit, fraud, confusion, trouble." *Barat* may have two sources, either ultimately the Greek verb *prattein* "to do business" or a more recent origin in the old Breton *brat* "betrayal, treachery."

Cabotage

Cabotage is a collective term for the maritime laws of an individual country that regulate coastal trade by ship within the legal territorial waters of that country. For example, a foreign-crewed and foreign-owned ship, without the proper permit, may not carry coastal cargo from one Canadian port to another Canadian port. The law is enunciated in this passage from the Canadian Coasting Trade Act: "no foreign ship or non-duty paid ship shall, except under and in accordance with a licence, engage in the coasting trade." New Zealand only permits cabotage if foreign ships take on a certain number of New Zealand nationals as crew or pilot. Sometimes, as happens with smaller nations, ships of domestic registry can't handle large cargo and so foreign ships under a cabotage permit are allowed to transport the goods.

The word cabotage, however, is becoming obsolescent, replaced by clearer phrases such as "coastal trading." Contrary to some dictionaries' assertions, cabotage is not based on explorer John Cabot's name. Giovanni Caboto was born in 1450 and sailed to the happy isles in 1499. But *caboteur*, naming a kind of boat, appears in written French as early as 1277. A *caboteur* is still used as the name of a wooden vessel that plies the coast, does not often venture into open sea, but sails from port to port as a cargo vessel.

It probably begins with the Latin word for the human head, *caput*. But even in classical Latin, *caput* had expanded meanings such as "headland of a peninsula." *Cabo* (from Latin *caput*) is a Spanish word for something jutting out, such as a headland, a point, or a cape of land thrusting into the sea. A form *cabotz* in Old Provençal (also from Latin *caput*) that meant "big-headed fish" or "tadpole," could have been a sailor's jesting term for any small boat. *Caboto* also may be an early Northern Italian dialect version of the surname *Caputo* "big-head." Early Northern French has *cabot, chabot* "a small vessel that slowly sails along a coast from headland to headland, from port to port." Modern English, French, and Italian now have *cabotage, cabotage,* and *cabotaggio* for "sailing along a coast in a trading vessel" and "coastal trade," to which a twentieth-century meaning has been added. Cabotage is allowing a country to regulate airplane traffic in its own skies and over its own territory.

Demurrage

When a chartered-by-contract ship is not returned to the owner on a specified, agreed-upon date, that owner could lose money on the next chartering of his vessel. This may occur in loading or unloading the cargo of a vessel. The days specified by the ship to load or unload are called "lay days." Exceeding them may invoke demurrage. The delay may be caused by circumstances not related to the charterer's action, such as ice-at-sea demurrage, or collision demurrage wherein time was lost performing repairs caused by a collision. The word has also been used in other industries that depend on the timely shipment of goods, such as truck transport and air cargo.

Therefore, maritime law provides a remedy, by which the owner can bring an action for recovery against the charterer, said recovery to consist of compensatory damages payable for lost time. From a 1755 manual of insurances comes this rule: "If the Delay was occasioned by the Merchant, he shall be obliged to pay for the Days of Demurrage, to the Captain." In English law, demurrage is taken as a daily rate and always as a fixed sum. The contracting parties agree in advance to "just in case" contemplated damage. From the standard legal authority Maritime Law, comes this explanation: "Demurrage is usually typically quoted at a certain rate per day and pro rata for a part day. If no limit is set to the number of days on demurrage, the ship owner is bound to keep the ship at the loading port as long as it is necessary for the charterer to load, or at least until commercial frustration overtakes their contract, since the charterer is paying extra for the privilege of detaining the ship. Commonly, however, a fixed number of days on demurrage is stipulated in the contract so that holding over longer is a breach of contract."

The word *demurrage* stems from a French verb *demeurer* "to rest, to stay, to delay, to hesitate." In older French, the verb had orthographic variants including *demorer, demourer, demurrer*. The noun harks back to the verb *to demur* < Classical Latin *demorari* "to tarry, to linger, to delay" whose root we see in a few other Latinate English words such as *moratorium* "period of delay" and in the legal term to register, to put in a demurrer, that is, to enter a delaying pleading by one party that says, "What the other party claims is true, but it is not of sufficient legal force and so this action should not be allowed to continue." In looser definition, demurrer is sometimes a synonym for objection or exception.

With those saliferous sea-words inspected and safely stowed, let's make for port where some tasty food terms await the homing sailor still abob on the ocean of language.

CHAPTER 4

Edible Words

Food words are as tasty as the comestibles they describe. To shuck the succulent oysters of etymology and expose the glistering innards of an everyday culinary term is a treat as delicious as swallowing the oyster itself. Like our foods, the English words we use to label our edibles have come from all over the earth and are often stuffed with surprise. I hope my plate will perk your verbal palate.

Calamari, Meet Calamity

Thanks to some scaly god of food names who watches over English menus, no restaurant is forced to offer seafood using the repellent syllables "chopped squid." There is something creepy and revoltingly tentacular about our word *squid*. Even tentacle is not something one wishes thrown around one's shoulders on a heavy beach date. *Tentacle* as a word is the English version of *tentaculum* (Modern Latin "little feeler"). Ewwww!

Calamari tastes better than squid. Calamari went to seafood school. Calamari is elegant and mysteriously Mediterranean in sound with its false echo of the Italian word for sea, *mare*. Who can say why? But we do know that food must have a tasty moniker, as well as flavor and "mouth-comfort" to use a weird phrase I once read in some commercial food-testing laboratory manual. In this chapter we soufflé and chew on such thoughts.

Culm

We all know the image: Huck Finn chewing on a hay stem. Huck is rolling across his lips a culm of timothy grass (hay). Generally, a culm is the stem of any grass, the aerial portion of the graminacious stem that grows above ground, the part of the grass stem we see. The culms of bamboo (yes, it's a giant grass!) are large and woody. The hollow culm of a tiny ditch grass may be narrow and flimsy. A few other kinds of plants have culms: sedges, rushes, and some other monocots. *Culmus* in Latin means "stalk, stem of grain." Other meanings of the lexical form *culm* exist in English, but today we treat only the grassy one.

Latin culmus is a shortened form of the root apparent in *calamus* "reed, bulrush" in which syncope (the loss of some internal letters of a word) has made off with the second unstressed vowel. Thus, CAL-a-mus is rendered by quick, assertive pronunciation into *calmus and then into culmus. While the intermediate form disappears, the original and the ultimate forms are both retained in the language and the newer, shorter form becomes available to expand Latin's vocabulary.

In Latin *calamus* means reed, stalk of a plant, straw, quill pen, arrow, fishing pole, or pipe. The Latin word was borrowed from Greek where *kalamos* means a reedpipe, a flute made from a reed, a pen, a cane of bulrush. The ancient Greeks also used *kalamos* to mean any plant that was not a tree or a bush. A feminine form, *kalame*, meant grass-stubble, cornstalk, fishing rod, remnant, and residue.

Calamari

Perhaps the most interesting English term derived from Latin *calamus* is that menu word for sliced, fried, squid, calamari. A dish of calamari also includes sliced, ring-shaped portions of the squid's body, not just the arms and tentacles. Before it's sliced up, the body does, in fact, look hollowed out, sort of like a reed.

Most squid have eight arms and only two tentacles.

Calamarius is a Latin adjective "pertaining to a reed pen." A *calamarius* is also a medieval Latin noun naming an occupation: a slave or monk writer (recording secretary) who uses a reed pen, a scribe or copyist. The neuter noun *calamarium* referred to a writing stand at which the scribe/monk stood or sat to make his copies of the work being reproduced. A *calamarium* was an ink horn or pen case, as reeds were then used as writing implements.

The chief question: how did the word's meaning jump from reed pen to squid? Well, squid's ink was used to make the writing ink into which a reed pen was dipped. And cephalopods such as squid have an internal flexible horny shell that is shaped like a pen. Take your pick. I say it's the squiddy ink. Ancient inks were indeed made from black squid liquid and from nutgalls and, for all I know, puppy dog tails.

The first printed form meaning squid appears in a fourteenth-century Italian dialect as *calamaio* or *calamaia*. Now *-aio* or *-aia* are Italian suffixes that produce indefinite nouns of numerical assembly such as *centinaio* and *migliaio*. So let's take a moment for a brief Italian lesson: *un centinaio di* means "about a hundred of." For example:

- *Arrivarono a centinaio.* "They came by the hundreds."
- The most frequent use of *un centinaio* is at Italian birthday parties where a shout of *"Un centinaio!"* means "may you live a hundred years or more."
- *Ci sono centinaia di cose a fare.* "There are hundreds of things to do."
- *Un migliaio di api svolazzano.* "There were about a thousand bees zipping all over the place."

Here's what these nouns of number mean:

- mille = 1,000
- Un migliaio = about 1,000
- migliaia = thousands

The zero grade of the Proto-Indo-European root *klh-mo- "grass, reed" has a reflex in ancient Greek *kalamos* borrowed into Latin as a word for reed or pen. An Indo-European cognate appears in Sanskrit, the principal language of ancient India, where *kalama* is a reed or a pen, as well as a sort of rice, that is, the seed of a reed-like plant. Attic Greek *kalamos* is cognate, too. Arabic borrowed its word for reed pen *qalam* from Greek. In turn, Swahili took *kalamu* "pen" from Arabic traders and slave-dealers hunting in Africa.

Other Familiar Words from the *Calamus* Root

One of the most famous horse-breeding properties in America is Kentucky's Calumet Farm near Lexington. A calumet is what early French explorers of the United States called an Indian peace pipe. Tobacco leaves were stuffed in the calumet's clay bowl and its narrow pipe was often made from a long, hollow reed. *Le calumet* is French from a medieval Latin diminutive of *calamus*, namely *calamellus* "little reed." American Indians offered the peace pipe to congenial strangers as a token of friendship, often to begin a bargaining session. Accepting an offered pipe implied that the person taking the pipe was open to peaceful negotiation.

Two technical terms in music history also derive ultimately from *calamus*. A shawm is a medieval instrument much like an oboe. Human breath moving over a vibrating double reed in the shawm's globular mouthpiece produces its characteristic sound. The broken route of the word's derivation, starting with Latin, looks like this: *calamus* Latin "reed" > *calamellus* Vulgar Latin "little reed" > *chalemel* Old French > Middle High German *schalmie* > Middle English *schallemelle* > Modern French *chalumeau* > Early Modern English *shawm*. Obviously, two prominent forms intermingled as the root rolled down through the centuries. In musicology, the lower notes of a clarinet's range are termed the chalumeau register.

Are the Words *Calamari* and *Calamity* Related?

Maybe. Some etymologists suggest that *calamitas* Latin "damage or disaster" arose from the noun *calamus* "straw, cornstalk" because disasters such as severe hailstorms or rainstorms or mildew infestations would have severely damaged ancient Roman crops including corn. The suffix *-tas* in Latin is used to make abstract nouns out of the simple semantic weight of a concrete word; all of which only implies *calamitas* ought to mean "the essential quality of a reed" or "the stalkiness of a cornstalk," both meanings of *very* limited use in a blunt language such as Latin. Thus, whatever metaphor once made *calamitas* mean "disaster" has been lost to word-searchers forever.

Peter Piper Picked a Peck of Pepper Words

Most of the words for pepper, in most of the languages of the world, hark back to a Sanskrit word *pippali* "long pepper." The famous English tongue twister relies on quick vowel alternations following plosives such as the letter /p/. Speedy transitions trip up the nimblest of tongues. But we are concerned with the Proto-Indo-European root of our word *pepper*. Its PIE zero grade was probably *-pip, perhaps onomatopoeic in origin, imitating the sound of the hot, spicy food being spit out upon an ancient eater's first tasting of a peppery morsel. One is reminded of other onomatopoeic instances such as ptui!, the mimetic word for the spitting out of fruit pits. Reflexes of PIE *-pip in Sanskrit also include *pippala,* the sacred fig tree of India, *Ficus religiosa,* also called the bo tree. By the time of Middle Indic there was a *pippari* form.

UNDER THE BO WITH BUDDHA

Ficus religiosa or *pippala* is the famous bo tree under which Siddhartha Gautama sat, awaiting enlightenment and Buddhahood. Compare the Sanskrit noun *bodha* "enlightenment." Students of Sanskrit will know that the name Buddha itself means "he who woke up."

Pep Rally

In high school, did you ever attend a football pep rally before a big game? If so, you used a word, pep, that can trace its ancestry back probably 3,000 years to the Sanskrit word under discussion here, namely, *pippali.*

A sports coach often delivers a pep talk before a big game to inspire his athletes. On the sidelines of the sports field or court assemble the pep squad of cheerleaders. This shortening of the spicy word *pepper* to suggest vim and vigor appears to be early twentieth-century American high school slang, first recorded in print in 1904.

Pippali = Pippari?

I have spoken before in my etymological ruminations about the l.r shift, a replacement ploy found around the entire world whereby the letter /l/ replaces the letter /r/ in a word, because it is easier for the speaker of a particular language to pronounce. This occurs both in borrowing across language family boundaries and also within language families themselves.

The l.r shift works the other way too: some replace /r/ with /l/. The best-known instance is a Chinese person learning English telling his English teacher that he must rock the door. "Rock" is easier for him to say than "lock." Linguists suggest that the Greeks in their travels, possibly under Alexander the Great who reached Sanskrit-speaking lands of ancient India, picked up the word and the pepper, but heard it as they wrote it in Greek, *péperi*. By the time it had settled pleasantly in Greece, *peperi* referred not to the long pepper but to the ground-up seeds of *Piper nigrum* (black pepper). From the Greeks, the Romans borrowed it early. Its form in Latin was *piper*, still with us in the botanical names of many peppers, such as *Piper nigrum*.

Many, many languages borrowed it from ancient Latin and Greek. A few are listed here:

- **Modern English** *pepper* < Old English *pipor* < *piper* Late Latin
- **Czech** *pepř* < *piper* Late Latin
- **French** *poivre* < *piper* Late Latin
- **German** *Pfeffer* < *piper* Late Latin
- **Finnish** *pippuri* < *piper* Late Latin
- **Ukrainian** *perets* < *piper* Late Latin

- Yiddish *fefer* < *piper* Late Latin
- Italian *pepe* < *piper* Late Latin
- Lithuanian *pipiras* < *piper* Late Latin
- Old Irish *piobhar* < *piper* Late Latin
- Welsh *pybyr* < *piper* Late Latin
- Arabic *al-filfil*< *peperi* Greek
- Hebrew *pilpel*< *peperi* Greek
- Turkish *biber* < *peperi* Greek
- Kurdish *bibari* < *peperi* Greek
- Georgian *p'ilp'ili*< *peperi* Greek
- Armenian *bghbegh* < *peperi* Greek

Note on the Arabic Word for Pepper

Arabic *al-filfil* "pepper" is also the source of perhaps the most familiar fast food of the Middle East, the falafel. The form *falafil* is the plural of the Arabic word *filfil* and means literally "peppers." Not every language in the world makes plural forms by adding /s/. Some Arabic nouns are pluralized by adding infixed vowels (the long /a/ in the middle of the plural form) and altering adjacent vowels, while not abandoning the consonantal root, in this case the borrowed root /f-l-f-l/.

Although there are many spellings, the English seem to favor felafil, whereas North Americans spell it falafel. The falafel takes many forms, but one of its earliest consisted of hotly peppered and spiced fried balls of chickpeas served in a pita bread sandwich. Bought off street stands today in Israel, Egypt, Jordan, Syria, Lebanon, often with a bit of salad tossed in, falafels are the street food of choice for the entire Middle East. And that's what's shaking with the pepper words.

ANTIQUITY OF PEPPER USE

Archaeological evidence proves that humans have been using pepper and grinding peppercorns for 9,000 years.

Lemon and Lime Are the Same Word

Both lemon and lime are derived from Arabic (*līmūn*) or Persian (*limou* "lemon"), but the earliest reflex of this root may be Indo-European. Thus, the words *lemon* and *lime* are not, as many dictionaries assert of "Middle Eastern" origin, but of South Asian provenance.

Sanskrit Nimbu or Nimbuka

In ancient India, the Sanskrit word for the Indian lime was *nimbū*, still used in Hindi. The Indian lime is a sort of cross between a lemon and a lime. *Nimbu pani* is a refreshing limeade drunk on a very hot Indian day. *Nimbu* may have been borrowed, as many Sanskrit terms were, into Persian as *limu*, and hence into Arabic as *līmīn*. Arabic has also *lima*, possible ancestor of lime, and a general collective plural form, *lim* "citrus fruits."

The path into English appears to have been: French *limon* < Spanish *limón* < Portuguese *limão* < Italian *limone* < Provençal *limo* < medieval Latin *limonem* < Arabic *līmūn* < Persian *limu* < Sanskrit *nimbū*.

In other Persian borrowings of Sanskrit words, initial Sanskrit /n/, unpalatable to the Persians, became an /l/ sound. And the Sanskrit /b/ is merely infixed and euphonic and dispensable (earlier Vedic Sanskrit form *nim'u*), because it was not needed in any Persian attempt at euphonious utterance. In Sanskrit and other Indo-European languages, a plosive such as /b/ sometimes replaces a glottal stop, represented here in *nim'u* by the superscript apostrophe. Putting the /b/ sound into the word makes the word easier to say, quicker to enunciate. Then the glottal stop itself is elided, thus *nimbu* became *limu*.

Further Borrowings

When some languages borrowed the word *limun* or *lime*, the forms were altered. For example, the Japanese word for lemon is *remon*, because /l/ is difficult for the Japanese to pronounce— Compare Japanese: *remon* "lemon" and Japanese: *raimu* "lime." One Chinese word for lemon *ning-meng* is an attempt at pronouncing a form of the word *lemon* borrowed from some language west of China. Mandarin Chinese gets a bit closer to "lime" with *lái méng*.

Note that English borrowed from French *limon* (fourteenth century) and *lime* (sixteenth century) and they became the yellow lemon and the green lime. Then in seventeenth-century French, another word that had been hanging around in French since the thirteenth century, originally borrowed from Latin, replaced both limon and lime first as the French scientific word and then as the popular French word. That word was *citron*. In modern French, lemon = *le citron* and lime = *le citron vert*. Lemon and lime, then, are related. Lemon made its way to English through Old French as *lymon* in the fifteenth century.

Lime first entered English in the seventeenth century, borrowed from a Spanish form, *lima*.

A Mess of Pottage: Exploring a Biblical Food Phrase

Recently, on the front page of a leading newspaper, a reporter had occasion to use an expression that signified selling something valuable at far too cheap a price. He referred to "a mess of pottage." But he or a copy desk editor felt it necessary to add an explanation of the phrase, in the belief that most readers would not understand it. Now the readership of this newspaper, it is safe to say, is among the most literate in the United States. So it interested me to see that this once well-known phrase is now largely unused, though met with now and then in expository prose.

Where in the Bible?

A mess of pottage is associated with the Bible, but does not appear in any text of any English Bible. It does appear in the heading to chapter 25 of the Book of Genesis in the Geneva Bible of C.E. 1560. In Genesis 25, Jacob and Esau were the twin sons of Isaac and Rebekah. Esau, all red and hairy, came out first. Firstborn of Isaac, Esau was the inheritor. However, the smarter Jacob tricked the hairy farmer Esau into giving up his half of the birthright. Jacob got Esau to sell his birthright for a mess of pottage, that is, a bowl of lentil soup. As an almost proverbial phrase, a mess of pottage came to mean "a real bargain, something valuable gained for almost nothing."

Esau's Foolishness and His Name's Origin

Later in Genesis, readers learn of another of Jacob's dirty tricks. With his mother's help, Jacob impersonates his hairy older twin by dressing in Esau's clothes and covering his own hands and the nape of his neck with the hairy hide of goats. Fooled by this ruse, their blind father, Isaac, is tricked into giving the younger son the blessing intended for the firstborn. Both Esau anecdotes in Genesis probably arose from the biblical etymology of Esau's name (not necessarily correct, as with so many Old Testament guesses at Hebrew etymology).

Esav is biblical Hebrew for "hairy" related to *se'ar* "hairy." Why was he an Edomite? Another name for the land of Edom was Seir. One etymology of Edom saw it as related to the Hebrew adjective *admoni* "ruddy, reddish" and *adom* "red earth of Israel"— incidentally the true origin of Adam, of Adam and Eve fame. God made Adam from the red earth of Israel. The King James Version reads: Genesis 25:29, "And Jacob sod pottage [boiled soup]: and Esau came from the field and he was faint [hungry]:

GENESIS 25:29–34 (KING JAMES VERSION)

—29 And Jacob sod pottage: and Esau came from the field, and he was faint:

—30 And Esau said to Jacob, Feed me, I pray thee, with that same red pottage; for I am faint: therefore was his name called Edom.

—31 And Jacob said, Sell me this day thy birthright.

—32 And Esau said, Behold, I am at the point to die: and what profit shall this birthright do to me?

—33 And Jacob said, Swear to me this day; and he sware unto him: and he sold his birthright unto Jacob.

—34 Then Jacob gave Esau bread and pottage of lentiles; and he did eat and drink, and rose up, and went his way: thus Esau despised his birthright.

GENESIS 25:29–34 (NEW INTERNATIONAL VERSION)
—29 Once when Jacob was cooking some stew, Esau came in from the open country, famished.

—30 He said to Jacob, "Quick, let me have some of that red stew! I'm famished!" (That is why he was also called Edom.)

—31 Jacob replied, "First sell me your birthright."

—32 "Look, I am about to die," Esau said. "What good is the birthright to me?"

—33 But Jacob said, "Swear to me first." So he swore an oath to him, selling his birthright to Jacob.

—34 Then Jacob gave Esau some bread and some lentil stew. He ate and drank, and then got up and left.

So Esau despised his birthright.

GENESIS 25:29–34 (COMPLETE JEWISH BIBLE)
—29 One day when Ya'akov had cooked some stew, 'Esav came in from the open country, exhausted,

—30 and said to Ya'akov, "Please! Let me gulp down some of that red stuff—that red stuff! I'm exhausted!" (This is why he was called Edom [red].)

—31 Ya'akov answered, "First sell me your rights as the firstborn."

—32 "Look, I'm about to die!" said 'Esav. "What use to me are my rights as the firstborn?"

—33 Ya'akov said, "First, swear to me!" So he swore to him, thus selling his birthright to Ya'akov.

—34 Then Ya'akov gave him bread and lentil stew; he ate and drank, got up and went on his way. Thus 'Esav showed how little he valued his birthright.

SOD:

- to boil, boil up, seethe, act proudly, act presumptuously, act rebelliously, be presumptuous, be arrogant, be rebelliously proud
- to act presumptuously
- to deal arrogantly
- to defy proudly

POTTAGE:

- boiled food, soup, pottage, thing sodden or boiled

The English poet George Gordon, Lord Byron, used the phrase mockingly in his poem "The Age of Bronze" lines 632–3: "Thou sold'st thy birthright, Esau! for a mess / Thou shouldst have gotten more, or eaten less."

Etymology of Pottage

The word came into English fifty years or so after the Norman Conquest. It's in print in a manuscript by C.E. 1200. In Anglo-Norman, Old French, and Middle French *potage* was any food cooked in a pot. During the next few centuries potage came to mean vegetable soup, then just vegetables. Today in modern French, for example, *le potager* is a vegetable garden.

Porridge is merely a sixteenth-century English variant of pottage. The first meaning of porridge in English was vegetable broth or soup, a stew of vegetables, herbs, or meat, thickened with barley. Only later did it come to mean boiled oatmeal served at breakfast.

Reversal Gag

On the principle that it is sometimes suitable to conclude with a cheap jest, here is a nifty note from Wikipedia: "By a conventional spoonerism, an overly propagandistic writer is said to have 'sold his birthright for a pot of message.' Theodore Sturgeon had one of his characters say this about H. G. Wells in his 1948 short story *Unite and Conquer*; but Roger Lancelyn Green (in 1962) ascribed it to Professor Nevill Coghill, Merton Professor of English Literature at the University of Oxford."

That's our pottage, not such a mess after all!

Cappuccino

Such bliss to be trendy! You sip a cappuccino on a Paris quai, languidly riffling through the foxed pages of your most recent incunabulary acquisition, a 1495 edition of Ovid's *Ars amatoria*, purchased from a bouquiniste's stall pitched on the parapets along the slow-flowing Seine. Past your table saunters a learned throng of students ambling toward the Sorbonne.

To your cappuccino-tasting companion, you comment on the origin of the coffee term, *cappuccino*. A cappuccino is a coffee drink made of espresso, steamed milk, and milk foam. Espresso is an Italian past participle meaning "pressed out" which was

the earliest meaning in English of the adjective "expressed."
A coffee making machine invented in Italy at the beginning of
the twentieth century contains a pump that presses or forces
hot water through fine-ground coffee. The expressed coffee is
thick and rich. Steamed milk foam is beaten into the espresso
and a daub of frothy, foamy milk from the top of the steaming
milk pitcher is floated on the surface of the coffee. That's a
cappuccino.

What a Little Hood!

In Italian, *cappuccino* means "little hood" or "little monk's
cowl." *Capucchio* is "hood" and *-ino* is a common Italian diminutive ending, hence "little hood." *Capucchio* is from Late Latin
cappa "cap, cape, hooded cloak, small head gear," possibly shortened from the Late Latin noun *capitulare* "headdress," ultimately
from Latin *caput* "head."

Cappuccino was first the Italian term for a Capuchin friar.
The color of the coffee reminded Italians of the brown robes
with pointed hoods worn by one of the Roman Catholic orders of
monks, namely the Capuchins. It is said the first cappuccino coffee served had little peaks of milky foam that looked like these
pointed hoods.

Sacrilegious Humor! Oh Dear!

This borrowing of a formal ecclesiastical term to name something
secular and lowly is part of the broad, quite healthy, anticlerical

humor that is widespread in Italy. Hundreds of words and phrases mock the omnipresent Roman Catholicism of Italy. My own favorite is the thick pasta called *strozzaprete* "priest-strangler" or "priest-choker." The joke is that the pasta is as thick as a penis, and that, because so many priests are gay, well . . . . The original meaning of *strozzaprete* in Italian street slang is simple: it's a vulgar comic synonym for "cock."

As one might imagine, Rome is the epicentre of these sacrilegious quakes. The hypocritical and licentious shenanigans of nuns and priests futtering in the shrubs of *la citta vaticana* have kept the temporarily eternal city laughing for centuries. We also find the feminine Italian word *cappuccina* "Capuchin nun." But on the Roman street it almost always means a salad of mixed herbs and is a not-too-sly reference to the supposed texture of a nun's unsullied pubic hair.

The Birth of an Order

The Capuchin order was founded by Matteo di Bassi of Urbino (died C.E. 1552), who, due to doctrinal spats, split from the regular Franciscans. The name refers to the pointed cowl or *capuche* worn by the brothers. The rule from 1529 emphasized the Franciscan ideals of poverty, austerity, and contemplative prayer. They were an important force during the Counter-Reformation. The severity of the rule has been somewhat mitigated, but they are still the strictest of the Franciscan orders.

Capuchin Franciscan friars have a sonorous Latin title worth saying aloud. Capuchins belong to the *Ordo Fratrum Minorum*

Capuccinorum, often abbreviated to O.F.M.Cap. "The Order of the Friars Minor of the Little Hoods."

EXTRA COFFEE NOTE

The etymology of the word coffee begins in an Arabic word for any prepared liquid, *qahwah*. It could mean wine or coffee. Turkish picked it up as *kahve* and applied it exclusively to thick Turkish coffee. Then Italians visiting Turkey borrowed it as *caffè*, and then the French as *café*, and the English as *coffee*—it flooded the world.

Say Cheese But Never Spray Cheese, Please

"Age is something that doesn't matter, unless you are a cheese," said American actress Billie Burke, defending her shocking longevity in show business. By the time Chaucer was writing *The Canterbury Tales* in Middle English, about C.E. 1385, our old word *cheese* was already well molded as *chese*. In this section we shall set forth plump rounds of verbal cheese lore including the fact that the white bloom on cheeses is in fact an antibiotic! Following the anfractuous twistings of the etymology of the word *cheese* down through linguistic history gives proof of how ancient and preferred a food it has been and continues to be.

Say "Cheese"

Middle English chese arose out of the Old English word *ciese* or *cese*, a close cousin of the modern German cheese word, *Käse*, one of the earliest words borrowed from Latin into a Germanic tongue. Linguists suggest the reconstructed West Germanic form was *kasjus, which in turn gave the Old Low German *kasi. They all stem from the common Latin word for cheese *caseus*. Our English word cheese has other close family members, among them the delightful *tsiis*, which is West Frisian, and Dutch *kaas*.

The great British etymologist Eric Partridge suggested a relationship of Latin *caseus* with Indo-European forms such as Old Church Slavonic *kvasu* "leaven, fermentation, fermenting agent" and a Sanskrit verb *kvathati* "it seethes, it ferments" and, clearly related, the Prakrit noun *chasi* "buttermilk." Perhaps more distantly related is the English word *whey*. In Old English, its form was *hwaeig* "whey" and in Gothic *hwathu* "foam, barm, froth." Prakrit, by the way, names several ancient Indic languages, vernacular descendants of Sanskrit. The Proto-Indo-European etymon was probably *kwat- whose verbal meaning was "to become sour, to ferment."

Also coined using the Latin word *caseus* was casein, the technical name for milk protein. Casein is broken in half by rennet in the production of cheese, forming curds and whey. It is an albuminoid that precipitates out of milk as curd. When further compacted by acid, curds of casein are the basis of cheese.

Cheese in Other Languages

Spanish took its cheese word, *queso*, directly from the earliest Latin word *caseus*. So did Portugese, as *queijo*. That's why many of us know the Mexican word for a little cheese turnover, *quesa-dilla*, a diminutive of *quesada*, a larger cheese turnover. But the other Romance languages did not borrow *caseus*. The so-called Romance languages evolved initially from the slangy street Latin of Roman soldiers posted on duty in Gall, in the Iberian Penin-sula and elsewhere. Consider that in French, cheese is *fromage*, in Italian *formaggio*, in Breton *fourmaj*, and in Provençal *furmo*. How did that happen? It concerns provisioning an advancing Roman army.

On their initial forays into darkest Gall and flamenco-prone Iberia, Roman soldiers had to be fed. One of the foods that accom-panied Roman legions on the march were great rounds of hard Roman cheese slung into bleached leather sacks on the backs of donkeys. This Roman cheese was nicknamed *formaticum* by the soldiers. *Caseus formatus* was cheese "formed" into wheels or rounds, molded, but not too soon moldy.

Now remember that the first documents that can be said to con-tain an Italian language were legal formulae from the region of Benevento that date from C.E. 960–963. By the time Italian was thus evolving, *formaticum* had lost its Latin neuter noun ending and its unstressed intervocalic /i/ and sounded like *format-cho*, not too far from its modern spelling of *formaggio*.

No, Really Say "Cheese"

Everywhere on this glum planet, photographers want camera subjects to smile. Smile. Always smile. Smile as your spouse heads for jail having been convicted of bestiality with an aardvark. Smile as the surgeon who has just sawed off your right leg asks for a Polaroid for the Hospital's Memento Album of Stumps. In order to produce that required smile, English-speaking photogs often give the command, "Say cheese." To smile requires the motion of about twelve facial muscles including the two most important, the levatores anguli oris. There is one levator anguli oris at each end of the mouth and each performs what its Latin name says it does: each elevates one corner of the mouth. Many other facial muscles take part in a genuine smile. Just for interest here is a doctor's list of the names of the thirty-six muscles of human facial expression:

- Auricularis anterior (2)
- Auricularis posterior (2)
- Auricularis superior (2)
- Buccinator (2)
- Corrugator supercilii (2)
- Depressor anguli oris (2)
- Depressor labii inferioris (2)
- Depressor septi nasi (1)
- Frontalis (1)
- Levator anguli oris (2)
- Levator labii superioris (2)
- Levator labii superioris alaeque nasi (2)
- Mentalis (1)
- Nasalis (2)
- Orbicularis oculi (2)
- Orbicularis oris (1)

- Platysma (1)
- Proccrus (1)
- Risorius (2)
- Zygomaticus major (2)
- Zygomaticus minor (2)

The (2) means the muscle is bilateral, one on each side of the face. The (1) means the muscle is solitary and unpaired. "It takes one more muscle to smile than to frown," states plastic surgeon David H. Song, M.D., F.A.C.S., assistant professor at the University of Chicago Hospitals.

Why do not only photographers, but those looking at the pictures afterward find it so easy to detect a fake smile? Because the phony smirk is only done with the mouth muscles. A genuine smile requires the eyes to crinkle in oogly-woogly warmth. When they don't, an onlooker can tell immediately. Many acting classes require students to spend an hour or two in front of a mirror making sure they master the "eye-smile."

But the French Say "*Ouistiti*"

"Say cheese" is the standard English instruction, but other languages have their own words to elevate those mouth-corners. My own favorite is the sweetly bizarre word usually employed in France, namely *ouistiti*. It has those lengthy /i/ sounds that require the lips to pull back in an obligatory smirk of pronunciation. *L'ouistiti* is a French word for a kind of marmoset, a small South and Central American monkey with goofy tufts of fur around its head. Its native name is said to be an imitation of the little monkey's characteristic alarm cry. Interestingly, marmoset began as a French word from a now obsolete medieval French term *marmouset* that meant "grotesque figure." There are other delights in the *ouistiti* term as well. Young French children find it a giggly word. The first part of the word sounds to Parisian kids like "*Oust!*" "Get lost! Scram!" and the last part -*titi* can mean a poor little orphan or can be French nursery talk for Mommy's breasts.

I Shudder to Bug You with More World "Cheese" & Smile Expressions

Surprisingly "cheese" as a smile inducer shows up in Japanese, pronounced chiizu. Arabic relies on the long, long Semitic /i/ sound in their word for apple, *seeeeb*. I'm exaggerating the number of e's in the word, and it is better transliterated as *sib*. The Chinese require those being photographed to say out loud, "eggplant," that is, in Chinese, *qeezee*. Also abounding in long /i/ sounds is another borrowing from English in most Latin American countries where the photographer says, "*Diga whiskey*" "say whiskey." If you are sandaling sportively along a beach in Rio and wearing the equivalent of a postage stamp to ensure modesty for your lean, bronzed bod, a Brazilian shutterbug might shout out, "*Olha o passarinho*." "Look at the little bird." Danish paparazzi may scream "*Sig appelsin*" "say orange." Thais ask the camera subject to say "Pepsi." Russians utter the phrase "*ska'zhite siski*" which means "say boobs." This makes Russians of all ages laugh—who can say why, tovarich? To get kids to smile, German photographers often ask them to say *"Spaghetti"* or *"Kaesekuchen"* "cheesecake."

Curd? What a Bunch of Crud!

The word *curd* appears to be derived from the form *crud*. In Middle English it was *crud*, then curd appears first in recorded form in the fifteenth century. As you may suspect, linguistics has a fancy name for almost everything that happens to letter sounds, phonemes, inside a word. When the /u/ and the /r/ of crud got switched to curd, the transposition of those letters is called metathesis, which is the Greek word for transposition. Greek *meta* = English across = Latin *trans*. Greek *thesis* = English "a placing" = Latin *positio* "a placing." Most etymologists claim ignorance of the ultimate origin of crud, because no similar root is known in Teutonic or in the Romance languages or in their mother tongue, Latin. But there is the Irish word for curd, *cruth*. And there is the Gaelic *gruth*. Are they the source of crud or early borrowings into Irish and Gaelic of an Old English word? We shall never know. Cruddy, ain't it?

Three Technical Words in Cheesemaking Worth Knowing

Hey, these words are not that obscure. Who knows? You could get trapped in a train wreck with 100 cheese makers on the way to a Mold Convention. Were I so trapped, I'd opt for euthanasia by limburger. But you might wish to live and talk to them. Then you'd need to know:

1. **Affinage**—borrowed from French, it means maturing and aging the cheese after you have made it. *L'affinage* means "finishing off." You can see within the word, *fin*, French for "end." Old French afiner "to bring to completion" entered early French from Late Latin *affinare* = the Latin prefix *ad-* "to, at" + *finis* Latin "end." The French agent nouns are sometimes used in English cheese making. The person in charge of aging cheeses is an affineur (male) or affineuse (female).

2. **Annatto**—a dye extracted from the waxy pulp and seeds of achiote, widely used in cheese making to give a red, yellow or orange color to cheeses that otherwise would tend to be a dull off-white color. Annatto is widely used today to give cheddar cheese its characteristic orange hue. It's one of the chief coloring agents in salad oils such as French dressing. There are about nine different spellings of annatto. Achiote is a Central American shrub or small tree (*Bixa orellana*) that early Spanish conquistadores discovered Caribbean islanders using to dye their bodies and to make male lipstick, hence one of the shrub's nicknames, "lipstick tree." Aztecs named it *achiotl*, in their language Nahuatl. In Mexico, achiote is an ingredient of *cochinita pibil*, the spicy pork dish so popular throughout the country.

3. **Bloomy rind**—Two of my favorite French cheeses are camembert and brie. For years I had to refer to the white,

powdery stuff on the outside of the little cheese rounds as "white, powdery stuff." You can imagine how chic and *soigné* I appeared at snooty wine-and-cheese tastings: "Did you hear that cloddish word nut? That rural boor actually said the brie was coated with white, powdery stuff. I mean, really, the depth of some people's ignorance!" Nowadays, deftly raising my tortoiseshell lorgnette to view the insulting person as one might examine a cockroach, I purr, "Oh Deirdre, don't you find the bloomy rind of that *Camembert de Normandie* simply too, too exquisite?" I have brought many a party to an utter standstill with that line, as cognoscenti hear the sentence and slowly move as far away from me as they can and still be in the party room.

Do you ever find yourself at a loss for words when attending a cheese-nibbling or a wine-tasting? Well, quail no longer. Now you can pipe up and proffer gems of info. Begin by remarking casually, "Did you know that the bloom on cheese is penicillin? Camembert and brie production involve spraying a water solution of the molds *Penicillium candidum* and *Penicillium camemberti* on the surface of the shaped cheeses and then leaving them to ripen for about three weeks." Believe me, with tidbits like that at your fingertips, you become a veritable magnet at parties. Fascinating strangers cluster to you, drawn like moths to the flame of knowledge. By the end of the party, personal operatives will invite you to weekends in Taos where you will visit svelte women at dusk and learn to play the guitar with your toes.

But why, you ask, is the white powdery stuff called *bloom*? Bloom's first meaning in English is "flower." Then the word takes on a veritable kaleidoscope of added meanings, including the crimson tint of milady's cheek and other flushes of color. The bloom on a maiden's peachy cheek is easily transferred to chromatic suffusions on other earthly objects. As early as C.E. 1639, bloom is used to describe the powdery whitish blue color on newly picked plums and grapes and other fruits. It was an easy transfer from the whitish bloom on fruit to the whitish bloom on cheeses.

CHAPTER 5

Word Words

Fear not, possibly daunted reader. You have bravely ventured this far into the darkest, thorn-strewn thickets of Casselmania and thus proven your readerly grit and spirit of inquiry. Now I offer the story of two technical terms in linguistics, schwa and calque. But, trust me still, o paragon of prowess, I shall not lead you astray into paths of complexity and torture. You speak schwas every hour of your life and thus it behooves you to know what a schwa is. They are friendly, modest little creatures who, if treated kindly, will take meat right out of your hand—seldom literally. So meet a schwa. Take one out for a treat, maybe a Slushy at your local Piggly-Wiggly?

Shake hands with the noble calque as well. Make her your constant companion along the pathway of language and you shall find the vista at trail's end as exciting as, say, a glow-in-the-dark painting on black velvet of Bernie Madoff warming a cup of borscht for the devil. Also on the verbal menu is the un-freaking-believable tmesis, nonce words, and my new origin of the current term *dude*.

Un-freaking-believable Is an Example of Tmesis

As we paddle our canoe along the mainstreams and backwaters of the American spoken word, we dock this time at an everyday figure of speech with an obscure name. The technical rhetorical term is tmesis: inserting a separate word into the midst of another host word, often a compound adjective. Abso-bloody-lutely! Well, la-de-goddamn-da! Any-old-way. Up-make-ya-barf-setting! I'm stony broke is transformed into: I'm stony-ass-hanging-out-broke. By the way, both the /t/ and the /m/ are pronounced in modern English, to give T-MEE-sis. The plural form is tmeses. In general, the inserted word or phrase appears just in front of the stressed syllable of the host word. In-freaking-credible, huh?

For those afraid they might swallow their widdle tongues trying to say any word that starts with /tm/, we have a nursery synonym. You can call it a sandwich term. But at least attempt to say tmesis and don't be so ri-goddamn-diculous.

Etymology of Tmesis

A direct borrowing from ancient Greek through Latin, tmesis means "a cutting," ultimately from the common Greek verb *temnein* "to cut." The vowel gradations /tom-/tem-/tm-/ of that verbal root are very productive of borrowed English words. The -tom stem appears in hundreds of English medical and scientific terms. When first named, an atom was something not able to be divided or cut from Greek alpha privative, a simple initial

/a/ meaning "not" + *tomos* "something cut." In its prime sense, anatomy first meant "cutting up" a dead body, from *ana* Greek "up" + *tomia* "a cutting." Appendectomy is made up of *appendix* + *ek* Greek "out" + *tomia*, an excellent word for surgical excision of the appendix. That wonderfully orotund monosyllable, tome, that names a large or ponderous book, originally referred to one volume in a multivolume set of books such as an encyclopedia, the tome being one of the volumes "cut" off when picked out from the set. A dichotomy was first a subject "cut" or divided into two (Greek *di*) often contradictory parts. A woman at troubled birth who needs an episiotomy receives a perineal incision, from *epision* Greek "pubic region" + *-otomy* Scientific Greek "incision but not removal."

In Latin the same root shows up in the Roman word for a barber, *tonsor* "a cutter (of hair)" and a monk's haircut, a tonsure, and in a silly, pretentious synonym for barbershop once popular in America, tonsorial parlor. The most intriguing reflex involves the history of an English word for a holy building, temple. It harks back to Latin *templum* whose earliest meaning was an area of cleared land marked off, cut off, by an augur as a place suitable for a religious ceremony, namely, an augury. The Latin word appears to be cognate with the Greek verb *temnein* "to cut" and its primordial meaning "land cleared of trees, land on which all the trees had been cut down." Only later in Roman history did *templum* come to refer to a building erected on such ground and consecrated to the worship of gods.

The Dreaded Tmesis

The first word in the title of this chapter is an expletive or scatological tmesis, in which an obscenity, or a substitute for an obsenity, is thrust into a word to perk up its vibrancy, to achieve a humorous effect of exaggeration, to grab the listener's attention, or to pump new life into an overused superlative adjective, as in this example of drill-sergeant English: "Out-mother-fucking-standing, Private Smith! Now let's see you drill a two-inch hole into this parade ground with your dick at full salute."

Some "experts" claim that insertion of an obscene infix such as fucking is only possible into adjectives or adverbs.

- That is un-fucking-believably stupid.
- That is un-fucking-believable stupidity.
- That is unbelievable stu-fucking-pidity.

This theory would have us believe that the third sentence is never heard. Several marines swear to have audited the third sentence and further attest, hands on noble hearts, that it aptly describes a good deal of military snafu heretofore filed under the rubric: Clusterfuck. In the humble opinion of your very devoted deponent (*moi*), the third sentence shows the most creativity and I would mark it "A" in my Dirty Writing class.

Other nifty tmeses include the following:

- Ala-fucking-bama from *My Cousin Vinny*
- Viet-fucking-nam! from *Forrest Gump*
- That makes him a lia-fucking-bility from *Boondock Saints*

Shakespeare Used Tmesis

"This is not Romeo, he's some other where," wrote the bard in *Romeo and Juliet*. It is best to keep tmetic infixation simple. Of course, it need not only transform adjectives. In older English, it was used to break up longer pronouns and even short nouns. "Whatsoever might please an editor" can be broken by tmesis into "What might be soever pleasing to an editor." "Be thou ware" could stand in for the command "Beware." All now sound and read as rather stuffy Victorian anachronisms. And yet, as a wise man may have said, "What place soever you may reach maketh fruitful the voyage."

Compound nouns can be split, as a critic noted when he asked readers to "forgive the quaint tmesis of his opening line: 'How bright the chit and chat!' " Here tmesis adds a pinch of salt to the shopworn word *chitchat*. "Where I go ever" once stood in poetry for "wherever I go." In his play *Richard II*, Shakespeare split the word however: "If on the first, how heinous e'er it be, To win thy after-love I pardon thee." In Shakespeare's *Troilus and Cressida* the reader finds "that man—how dearly ever parted."

Complex Tmesis

Complex punning tmeses are possible, but tricky to comprehend on first reading. It's a shame James Joyce did not indulge, although *Finnegans Wake* has some Joycean blends that properly count as tmetic. One punning tmesis of my own devising depends on knowing that the adjective *exsanguinating* means "bleeding to death, losing massive amounts of the red stuff." Thus a weary intern, at the end of an all-nighter in a London hospital's E.R. might complain, as he watched another gurney being wheeled in bearing an accident victim, "Not another ex-bloody-sanguinating punter!" Punter is British slang for customer.

Within the bounds of tmesis, gradations of off-color speech may exist. Consider the Cockney adjective "abso-fuckin-lutely," in its minced form used in the lyrics of one of the songs in the Lerner and Loewe musical *My Fair Lady*: "abso-blooming-lutely." When Eliza Doolittle sings this, the lyric of the song is actually quoting Bernard Shaw's original stage play *Pygmalion* written in 1915 and first staged in 1916. During that period of Edwardian prissiness in London, even a rebel like Shaw dared not use the original he had heard once when visiting a fruiterer at Covent Garden Market.

TUMBARUMBA: An Aussie Name

In Australia, tmesis is popularly called tumbarumba. Tmetic infixation is common in Australian street talk. Tumbarumba is an Australian town featured in a familiar poem titled "Tumba Bloody Rumba" by John O'Grady, a bit of poesy that features several tmeses such as "e-bloody-nough" and "kanga-bloody-roos."

During the first run of the modern British teledrama "Cold Feet" the character Rachel made tmetic praise a national catch-word when she kept saying, "Fan-bloody-tastic!" Of course, that was across the pond on "a whole nother network" (tmesis of another).

Tmesis may also slice into the middle of some geographic names quoted in a pejorative sense. "Why bother fishing in the Susqua-doggone-hana? No fish worth eatin' in that stream."

Clearly, wherever English is spoken on this spinning orb, the use of tmesis is not obsolete. It is a-freaking-live and a-fucking-bundant.

In Awe of a Schwa

Schwa is the most common vowel sound in the English language and yet few English speakers are able to name it. True, schwa is a term in linguistics, not obscure to linguists, but almost unknown outside of phonology. It is the very weak, unstressed vowel sound you hear at the beginning of the English words along and alone, a soft "uh" sound. In the word *sofa*, the final syllable is a schwa. Schwa, pronounced /shwa/ in English, rhymes with paw. Its symbol in the International Phonetic Alphabet (IPA) is a reversed lowercase /e/ that is ə. Schwa in English sounds like a very weak, unstressed short /u/.

Here are examples from English with the stressed syllable marked with an acute accent and the schwa syllable unmarked:

- bútton
- óven
- trústful
- cóusin
- stómach
- abóve

- dózen
- adjúst
- confrónt
- táken
- péncil
- supplý

Schwa can be spelled with different vowels. It is spelled <a> in above, adjust, and stomach; <e> in oven and dozen; <i> in cousin; <o> in confront; and <u> in trustful.

Origin of the Word Schwa

The word *schwa* was borrowed into English from German, where it was borrowed from the name of a Hebrew grammatical sign that resembles our colon, that is, : called *shevá*.

Shevá or *sh'va* in Hebrew is a sign placed under a consonant to show the supposed absence of a following vowel sound. The name of this Hebrew sign is written *Schwa* in German, and schwa in English.

Shva or *shaw* in Rabbinic Hebrew means "the emptiness, the nothingness, or nought." It is pleasing that the Hebrew word itself contains the *shevá* sign under its first letter called *shin*.

The Story of the Word Shibboleth

This is a bit of biblical trivia about the Hebrew letter *shin*. In the biblical book of Judges 12:6, we read about the tribe of

Ephraim who did not have the sound of the letter *shin* in their dialect of Hebrew. Thus they could not easily differentiate between the sound /sh/ represented by the Hebrew letter *shin* and the sound /s/ of the Hebrew letter *sin*.

Once upon a time these Ephraimites were at war with the neighboring Gileadites. The Gileadites did have the sound /sh/ in their Hebrew words. Both tribes were of similar appearance, so the Gileadites devised a way to check for spies and intruders. They asked everyone they suspected of being an enemy or enemy spy to pronounce the Hebrew word *shibolet*.

Those of Gilead picked the word because it has a *shin* at the beginning of the word and was very difficult for the Ephraimites to say properly. They might have selected any Hebrew word beginning with "sh." *Sibolet* happens to mean "ear of corn, seed head of any grain plant, etcetera." An Ephraimite would say "sibolet" instead of the correct "shibolet" and thus get caught and perhaps put to the sword.

Shibboleth in English and in other European languages came to mean a word that can be used to distinguish one group from another. Developed meanings of shibboleth include platitude, a distinguishing custom, a catchword, or a slogan.

Modern Example of a Shibboleth

During World War II, a propaganda comic strip booklet was printed by the United States Department of War. Yes, the material was racist. After all, North America was at war with Japan. The brochure was part of a seventy-five-page propaganda pamphlet called *Pocket Guide to China*. Its most infamous section was "How to Spot a Jap." In 1944, that section was removed from the *Pocket Guide to China*.

But what we are interested in is the modern use of shibboleths as test words during war. Ordinary Japanese soldiers who had been taught to speak English, to impersonate Japanese-Americans, were likely to mess the pronunciation of some words. Lalapalooza was one. It was likely to come out of a Japanese soldier's mouth as "ra-ra-pa-rooza." It's been reported that, halfway through the mangling of the word, sentries shot to death the person uttering the test word.

LIVE LONG AND PROSPER!

In Judaism the letter *shin* also stands for the word *Shaddei*, one of the names for God. When a Hebrew *kohen* or priest recites the Priestly Blessing, he forms the letter *shin* with his hands. In the mid-1960s, actor Leonard Nimoy used a single-handed version of this gesture to create the Vulcan Hand Salute for his character, Mr. Spock, on the TV drama *Star Trek*.

Causes of Schwa-ification

Unstressed, quickly said vowels may have a shortened lifespan. For example, in several British dialects, the word *medicine* has only two sounded syllables, due to exaggerated stress on the first syllable: MED-sin. The third syllable of medicine is first, a schwa, produced by a low-level phonetic rule that reduces unstressed short vowels, but second, the schwa can become so abbreviated that it disappears. In North American pronunciation the initial syllable of medicine is not stressed as strongly. Thus the second syllable survives and is pronounced, and medicine then has three sounded syllables.

This phenomenon of schwa-like disappearance produced one of the best extraphonological uses of the term *schwa* that I ever remember reading. It was the review of a bad play by an acerbic theater critic in an upscale magazine. The critic wrote, about one of the secondary actors in the fiasco, "the actor playing the son became a histrionic schwa. He disappeared. While on stage. No mean feat."

The schwa-ification rule accounts for transformations in many polysyllabic Latin words as they evolved into the Romance language forms of French, Italian, and so on. For example, Latin *bene* adverb "well" > Vulgar Latin *bene* > Romanz (earliest French) *ben* > modern French *bien*. Or the Latin *solus* "alone, single" > Vulgar Latin *solu* > Romanz *sols* > early French *solǝ* > French from C.E. 1175 *seul* "alone."

To Sniff or to Sniffle at the Question of Iterative Verbs

In the study of words, nouns and adjectives tend to have anecdotes attached to their derivations and, therefore, nouns and adjectives receive the most etymological attention. But English verbs have their own fascinating history, which I hope to prove in this peek at a not-very-well-known class of English action words called iterative verbs. Any explanation of iterative verbs is omitted from most discussions of English grammar, so you will be one-up on glum grammarians after reading this lighthearted once-over.

Chat or Chatter? Wrest or Wrestle?

Iterative means "repeating." It is an aspect of the verb that denotes continuously repeated action. You might sniff a flower. But if you sniffle while weeping, you sniff repeatedly. You may chat with a friend. But you chatter in idle gossip, blabbing away in a repetitive and possibly annoying manner. A bird may nest in a tree. But you might nestle down (that is, make many repeated "nesting" movements) in a goose-down duvet for a comfy evening by the fireplace. The faucet may drip drop by drop. But, in a fit of roaring anger, you may dribble saliva on your beard, repeatedly spritzing drips as you rant.

As you can see, the most frequent ways to form an iterative verb in English are to add a suffix -le or -er. Here are some iterative verbs with their root verbs:

- to bat > to batter
- to bob > to bobble
- to climb > to clamber
- to crack > to crackle
- to crump > to crumple
- to curd > to curdle
- to dab > to dabble
- to daze > to dazzle
- to flick > to flicker

- to float > to flutter
- to hop > to hobble
- to pat > to paddle
- to scrape > to scrabble
- to spark > to sparkle
- to suck > to suckle
- to top > to topple
- to twink > to twinkle
- to wrest > to wrestle

Many newer iterative verbs have no regular simpler verb in their ancestry, but are formations based on echoic roots, as babble, cackle, gabble, giggle, guggle, and mumble.

Iterative is the new adjective. Formerly the accepted phrase was frequentative verbs. But that was too clear a designation, having the understandable and descriptive "frequent" contained in the actual adjective. Thus, some linguistics scholar who wanted a minor aspect of English verb formation to appear much more complicated and abstruse than in fact it is, decided to use a more obscure adjective, iterative.

An Oxford Error? My Goodness!

In the prestigious *Oxford Companion to English Literature*, editor Tom McArthur opines from his solemn throne of toplofty authority, "There is only one iterative element in English, the suffix -le." My assessment of Mr. McArthur's magisterial certitude may be stated in six syllables: poo-poo, ka-ka, doo-doo.

Tell me then, Wee Tommy Know-It-All, where does that leave the clearly iterative use in English of the verbal suffix "er" as in float > flutter and state > stutter and blab > blabber? Well, that leaves -er as a prominent English iterative suffix, and that leaves Mr. McArthur wrong, or, to coin a silly phrase more suited to the upper realms of semi-ignorant linguistic claptrap, that leaves the dithering Mr. McArthur in a considerable state of counterfactual goofitude. As you may be able to discern through your pince-nez, Mr. McArthur, I found your hoity-toity tone in the OCEL quite nettlesome, dense as it was with personal opinion not clearly labeled to separate it from linguistic fact.

THE ITERATIVE OUT ON ITS ASS, ALAS!

You may have noted that I said we formed iterative verbs. Deliberate was my use of the past tense, for the verbal iterative suffix is obsolete in modern English. Nowadays it is far commoner to use adverbs and adverbial phrases to indicate the repeated action of a verb.

As partial proof, I quote from a reasonably authoritative tome published by your very own company, the *Oxford English Dictionary*'s head word entry: "-er, suffix forming frequentative vbs. The vbs. of this formation which can be traced in OE. have the form -rian (:OTeut. -rôjan); e.g. *clatrian* CLATTER, *flotorian* FLUTTER . . . . Further examples in Eng. are batter, chatter, clamber, flicker, glitter, mutter, patter, quaver, shimmer, shudder, slumber."

So much for Mr. McArthur's pomposity.

St-st-st-studying the Iterative Verb *Stutter*

The few dictionaries that bother with etymology proclaim that stutter is a frequentative or iterative verb from the obsolete English dialect verb *to stutt*, itself from Middle English *stutten* "to stutter," ultimately from the same Old Teutonic root as the modern German verb *stossen* "to strike against, to collide." Yeah? Maybe. But even the *Oxford English Dictionary* takes the trouble to point out how surprisingly late in the history of the English language the verb *stutter* appears.

YOU BIG ABLAUT!

Ablaut or vowel gradation is just the fancy term in linguistics when various causes force a root vowel to change slightly in Indo-European languages. A familiar ablaut or vowel grada-tion in English is the one that occurs in Germanic strong verbs such as English *sing, sang, sung,* where the morphological altering of the vowel affects the meaning of the verb. Ablaut here changes the temporal aspect of the verb. *Sing* is present, whereas *sang* and *sung* describe singings that took place in the past.

Its late appearance in English (C.E. 1570) makes me wonder if we are looking at a word with double sources: the standard Teu-tonic one as given above and a second independent frequentative formation from the verb *to state* "to utter words." To stutter in my suggested etymology, would be an iterative of *to state*, complete with ablaut or vowel gradation of the /a/ to a shorter /u/. So the speech line might have looked like this: *state* > **statter* > *stutter*. The intervening form is not attested in print.

Gone and Also Forgotten

In the list of iteratives above, you will have noted that a few of the shorter verbs are unknown to you. In the dice roll of language, some words win and endure to the end of talking; others lose, no sooner spoken than withered on the same tongue. Let's look at a few.

In Middle English *to twink* meant "to wink" from the same root as German *zwinken* "to wink." When polished gold flashed under royal candlelight, it winked and twinked many times and so the iterative verb *twinkle* was born. Gold doubloons twinkling in a pirate's chest of pelf might suggest that a fair damsel's eyes could twinkle too, and so they did, in the hope of appropriating some of the pirate's gold in mid-twinkle!

To bristle originally was said of hair that stood on end like the stiff hairs on a hog's back and sides, the same hairs that brush makers collected to make hard brushes. The root noun is lost except in manuals of ancient and recondite Scottish ritual where the questing word maven will discover the form *birse* and a ritual procedure called "licking the birse." When one assumed the high office of "soutar of Selkirk" (don't ask!) one had to pass through one's mouth a tidy bouquet of hog bristles. In Old English this was a *byrst*. It may have been a verb too. To stick up like many hog hairs then was to bristle. The word is in iterative form in Medieval

Dutch *borstel*, so English may have borrowed the verb already in frequentative aspect.

To crumple is an iterative form of the obsolete verb *to crump* "to curl up," so if you press paper into a tight ball, you are certainly crumpling it up. Crump is a direct relative of the German verbs *krummen* and *krumpen* "to shrivel up" and of a modern German verb from cloth making, *krumpfen* "to preshrink a garment before selling it." Also lurking in the same neck of the verbal woods are the forms *cramp*, *crimp*, and *crumble* "make into little crumbs."

Our valedictory wave to iterative verbs might be to wonder if we could revive the form. Do we need a verb to mean "commit many stumblebum acts while president"? That verb would be *to Bushl*. Darn, that form is taken. Then how about a verb that means "to stuff your body full of liver-destroying anabolic steroids"? That verb might be *to olympl*. Or every four years, we could just shrug our shoulders and shout, "Let the injections begin!"

A New Etymology of the Word *Dude*

All British and American dictionaries claim to be baffled by the origin of the word *dude*. Well, I think I have found a cogent source. Dude suddenly appears in print in the 1870s naming a man who dresses with too much attention to current fashion and thus exposes himself to the charge of being unmanly, even effeminate. One of the first appearances of the word is in a letter written by famed American artist of the Old West, Frederic Remington, in 1877, asking a friend for recent drawings: "Don't send me any more women or any more dudes. Send me Indians, cowboys, villains, or toughs."

The word *dude* eventually replaced dandy, an earlier term for a foppish male. In an 1878 book, *Fighting Indians*, natty, too dapper foot soldiers at Fort Snelling, Minnesota, are laughed at: "Company C, 20th Infantry, was at the time composed of dude soldiers, pets of dress parade officers." Fifty years later this western use of dude as a put-down to prim men from the Atlantic states, sucky tenderfoots who had never stepped in a fresh cow flop, survived to give us the term *dude ranch*, a holiday place where Easterners could go to learn to ride a horse and shake the loathsome label *dude* off themselves. Sissy lispers and quivering milquetoasts could hope for two-week metamorphoses, after which they would emerge from dude ranches to become tough, leather-lunged Marlboro men who stomped the earth like studs and died of cancer from smoking, puking their cowboy guts out. What a bunch of men, pardners!

Mark Twain Knew Dudes

Novelists of the time liked the word too. Mark Twain, who paid very careful attention to the American street speech of his day, uses the word in *A Connecticut Yankee in King Arthur's Court* (1889) to draw attention to the difference between stodgy British talk and lively, new American English: "Reverence for rank and title . . . had disappeared, at least, to all intents and purposes. The remnant of it was restricted to the dudes and dudesses." Mark Twain's brilliant criticism of western politics, the chief theme of *A Connecticut*

Yankee, is alive and thriving today among educated Americans. But Twain's coinage, a female dudesse, did not catch on.

However, 100 years later, in the mid-1970s a reader can find dudes and dudettes in hippie novels and pro-dope memoirs. Among the "love" generation of the 1970s and later, dude obtained its most generalized meaning, namely a male or female person. Dude also began toward the end of the twentieth century to replace the non-genderized collective "guys" as in this common valedictory line, spoken to a party room of girls and boys, "Gotta split. See you dudes later."

The Dudest Dude of Dudedom

An additional semantic layer was applied to the word *dude* at the turn of the twenty-first century where dude becomes a kind of adolescent male's ideal of the irresponsible boy-man. A perfect instance of this type of dude is the Jeff Bridges movie *The Big Lebowski* in which Bridges plays a shiftless, White Russian-guzzling slacker who calls himself and is called by others "The Dude." He represents a not-very-bright teenage boy's idea of maturity at a time of absolutely no adult responsibility of any kind, a hobo heaven kind of life, a dudehood where one can tool around Los Angeles wearing a yellowed T-shirt that has not been washed for two months and still have women fall at one's unwashed feet heaving with lust. Is dudehood attractive? Well, the film was not a money success on its first release, but it now has attained a cult status that permits annual Lebowski Fests in Louisville and other cities.

The Origin of Dude

Earlier suggestions for the source of the word *dude* are that it arose from a clothing term, *dud*, or *duds*, meaning men's clothing, or that it is based on a Dutch word for fool. No proof of either guess exists. The citation of use that caught my eye was in Booth Tarkington's 1899 novel *The Gentleman from Indiana* in which the extension of the noun to become a verbal phrase occurs: "Why should Cale Parker be wearing a coat, and be otherwise dooded and fixed up beyond any wedding?"

Dooded or duded up. Does that not suggest an origin in a slang past participle of the verb *to do*? A dude was a man *do-ed up*, meaning "all done up." All *do-ed up* is a recorded semiliterate variant of "all done up." The passive further hints that the poor overdressed male creature was acted on by women. No peacock, showoff masculine urge caused the male to don fancy pants. No, it was the overdressing hand of a fashionable woman, tempting sapper of male strength, civilizer of male rowdiness. A dude has been done, has been do-ed, all dolled up prissily like a fancy figure that a girl might place lifeless beside a dollhouse, that is, according to some women, perfect husband material.

Calque Me, Dude: How to Add New Words Instantly

A calque is an interlingual loan-translation, the literal translation, element for element, of a word from one language into the lexicon of another, using not the roots of the originating language but the roots of the borrowing language. Calque is the term used in philological studies and in linguistics. Calque was borrowed into English from French linguistics where it means literally "a copy of something," from the French verb *calquer* "to trace a design."

French borrowed the verb *calquer* from one Italian writer, the architect, artist, and biographer of painters, Giorgio Vasari, who used *calcare* in C.E. 1550 to mean "standing on a drawing and with one's *calx* (Latin, "heel of the foot") holding tracing paper over it and making a copy." The original Latin verb *calcare* meant "to tread on." The magnificent, resonant Italian title of Vasari's magnum opus is worth quoting: *Le Vite delle più eccellenti pittori, scultori, ed architettori* which means *The Lives of the Most Excellent Painters, Sculptors, and Architects.*

Skyscraper and Its Calques

A common example of a much-calqued term is the English word *skyscraper* meaning "a very tall, multistoried modern building." Skyscraper began in British naval vocabulary, at the end of the eighteenth century, as the name of a triangular skysail on a clipper ship. These high sails that some skippers set above the royals were also called moon rakers.

Once skyscraper also named a tall horse, a tall man, and a tall hat. By 1886 it was a slang term in American baseball for a high-flying hit. Skyscraper shows up in sports reports about cricket matches too. So the word was in wide use in American English when about 1880 it began to be employed to describe very tall new buildings, first in Chicago. People liked the word. Skyscraper sounded modern, vibrant, catchy. Soon it spread to other languages and was calqued. *Calque* is a noun and a verb, both transitive and intransitive.

The French *gratte-ciel* is calqued on the word *skyscraper*. *Gratter* is a French verb that means "to scrape" and *ciel* is French for "sky." In a similar manner, the Spanish calque for skyscraper is *rascacielos*, Portuguese *arranha-céus*, Romanian *zgârie-nori*, and Italian *grattacielo*.

PHRASE CALQUING

Individual words are calqued. So are phrases. English "that goes without saying" is calqued on the common modern French phrases "*cela va sans dire*" or "*ça va sans dire*." Both mean, "it is evident, it is clear, it is axiomatic."

The Difference Between a Calque and a Translation

Typically fuzzy and wrong, the Wikipedia entry on calques states that "Rest in Peace" is a calque of the Latin *Requiescat in Pace*. No, it is not a calque. "Rest in Peace" is a translation of the Latin epitaph. A calque is not a translation. A calque creates a new word or new phrase in a language. The French neology *gratte-ciel* is a calque, not a translation of the English word *skyscraper*. The phrase "rest in peace" does not create any new word. Both differ from direct word loans. *Le sweater* and *le parking* are direct loans into modern slangy French from English. They are not calques and they are not translations.

Wikipedia blathers on in error claiming that French *haute résolution* calques English *high resolution*. No, it does not. It is a translation. No new word or even meaning is created in this simple translation. All the meanings of *haute* and *résolution* were available in modern French, before the translation occurred. The differentiating concept does not seem like rocket science, but the bungling bozos who merrily steal others' work to compose their dud Wiki articles cannot apparently perceive the difference.

A Synonym for Calque

The most-used synonym for calque is the phrase *loan-translation*, itself an English calque of a term from German linguistics, *Lehnübersetzung* from *Lehn* German "loan" + *Übersetzung* "translation." Just to demonstrate the interplay of European languages, the German noun *Übersetzung* is itself a pre-medieval calque based on some long-forgotten German monk (perhaps) taking the Latin components of the Roman noun *translatio, translationis* and calquing them into German roots, thus: *trans* Latin "across" = *über* German "across, over, above" + *latio, lationis* = *Setzung* German "a placing, a setting." The original semantic flavor then of the word translation was "carrying or setting across languages a word meaning."

MORE CALQUES

Modern Greek takes the English word football and calques it as Ποδόσφαιρο from *pous, podos* "foot" + *sphairos* "sphere, ball." Likewise with the English word *Internet,* calqued in modern Greek as Διαδίκτυο, *dia* = inter (Latin "between, among") = "through, between, connecting" + *diktyo* "net."

Historical Example: Spanish Grandees Lust for Pale-Skinned English Beauties

The English phrase "blue blood" is borrowed from Spanish. Blue blood is a loan-translation, a calque, of the Spanish phrase *sangre azul* = *sangre* Spanish "blood" + *azul* Spanish "blue." Darker-skinned than Englishmen, Spaniards, very early in European history, remarked on the white skin of English women and found noteworthy the bluish veins visible through their fair skin—hence blue bloods. Arterial blood cells, loaded with oxygen, are red; venous blood, having given up its oxygen and now returning to the heart and then to the lungs to receive fresh oxygen, is a darker, bluish-red. The faint-red hue of venous blood is absorbed by the vascular wall of the vein and by the epidermis through which its color must pass to be seen externally, hence blue-blooded Brits.

An English phrase calqued from Spanish is "moment of truth," from *el momento de la verdad*, a bullfighting term. Spanish calques come from English too, and include modernisms with *hombre rana* "frogman," *lavaplatos* "dishwasher," *luna de miel* "honeymoon," *salvaje Oeste* "Wild West," *disco duro* "hard disk," and *banco de datos* "data bank."

O Obstinate Kraut!

In a calque, the elements or roots of the word in a foreign language are identified and then translated into the native language using native, not foreign, roots. Most languages of Europe borrowed some form of the word *television* directly; here are some examples:

English: I am watching television.
Italian: *Sono guardando la televisione.*
Spanish: *Estoy viendo la televisión.*
Finnish: *Olen television äärellä.*
Czech: *Já jsem před televizí.*
Polish: *Jestem oglądanie telewizji.*

Always obstinate, German took the root elements of the word *television*, namely *tele* Greek "far" + *visio, visione* Latin "a seeing" and translated them into good, sound, pure, non-foreign, Aryan Teutonic roots, to arrive at the cumbrous, ugly modern German word for television set, *Fernsehapparat. Mein Gott!* It consists of *fern* German "far" (translating the Greek tele) *sehen* German "a seeing" (translating the Latinate *vision*) and adding *apparat* "set" or "machine."

But often the German language's proud search for pure Teutonic roots ends with German embarrassment. Remember the trouble they got into with that concept under the Nazis? Nazi propaganda even came up with a word that covered the calquing of foreign words into pure Aryan German. That now discredited word was *Deutschifizierung* "Germanification," said to have been coined by the subhuman lizard creep himself, Paul Joseph Goebbels, Reichsminister of Propaganda from 1933 to 1945. I void my spittle on his memory.

In their horror of using a foreign element in their word for television, the Germans ended up with *apparat*, which is of course from the Latin noun *apparatus*. *Aber das ist schrecklich!* Because, *Mein Führer*, I don't sink zat zuh Romans were even Aryans! *Himmeldonnerswetter!*

The Nazi goofiness about purity of language ought to be a warning to all solemn conclaves who seek to legislate and bully a living language. It's always a tricky procedure, prone to dud-lumped fiasco. Just ask *L'Académie française* and observe their fruitless attempt over the years to keep English words out of modern French. I guess that's why, all over Paris, one hears Parisians using words such as *ketchup, steak, sandwich, tour operator* and *le club hot. Mais oui*, that fascist list of *L'Académie française* really works. Not.

Of course, German has given us some dandy words too. George Bernard Shaw introduced the term *superman* into English. He calqued it, having found the German word *Übermensch* in the writings of the German philosopher Friedrich Nietzsche. *Übermensch* is a noun compounded of *über* German "above, over, super" + *Mensch* German "person, man, human being."

English Calques from Chinese

English has translated many Chinese word elements into English word elements when borrowing terms and concepts from Chinese. Here are a few:

1. English *running dog* calques Chinese: *tsou gou* "hunting dog"—This phrase meaning "servile lackey" or "cringing

lickspittle toady" entered English through Washington military jargon. It is a metaphorical cliché of Chinese Commie balderdash featured in "Red" phrases such as "the running dogs of decadent capitalism."

2.   English brainwashing calques Chinese: *hsi nao* "wash-brain"— During the Korean War, United States Army doctors introduced knowledge of this mental torture procedure, in which prolonged force of various kinds is used to make prisoners give up their basic moral tenets and adapt Commie notions or insidious enemy ideas.

3.   English "long time no see" is a calqued phrase literally translated from Mandarin Chinese: *hao jiu bú jiàn.*

Nostalgia Calqued from German *Heimweh*

Algos is one of the Greek words for pain, and *-algia* is a frequent terminal in medical words describing various pains. Consider *neuralgia* "nerve pain" or, the one I use the most, *pygalgia* "a pain in the ass." The most familiar English word with the root is *nostalgia*. In ancient Greek *nostos* meant "a return home." Homecoming is the principal theme of the greatest ancient Greek story, *The Odyssey*. The Trojan War is over and Odysseus fights to journey home.

Curiously enough, the word *nostalgia* was not conceived by the Greeks. It is a loan-translation from the German word *Heimweh* "painful longing for home, homesickness." Johannes Hofer, a Swiss medical student, coined *nostalgia* in 1688 in a paper titled

"Dissertatio Medica de Nostalgia, oder Heimwehe" "a medical treatise concerning Nostalgia or Homesickness."

Well, kiddies, I calque-ulate that here endeth our terse scrutiny of this topic. Our lesson: linguistic chauvinism in the form of keeping your own language pure and free of all horrid, foreign, borrowed terms is a greased sidewalk. Once you take the first censoring step, you'll be on your ass faster than you can blink.

Nonce Words, not Dunce Words: Some New American Coinages

Some neologies (*neos* Greek "new" + *logos* Greek "word, study") are coined as short-lived jokes. But if there lurks within the freshly minted word or phrase some tang of widespread appeal, then the fragile neology—they can die overnight—may last longer than a day and endure to become more than a mere ephemeral fly-by-night and instead lodge firmly in our word hoard to become part of standard spoken English. I believe some of these new gems deserve an extended stay among us. Read about them and see if you agree.

Ambimextrous and Cinco de Marcho

Ambimextrous is an adjective that refers to an eater of popular food who will buy at Taco Bell or Taco Bueno indiscriminately. This comic coinage was formed on the analogy of the word *ambidextrous*, an anatomically strange word that literally means that both (Latin *ambi-*) one's hands are right hands (Latin *dexter* "right-handed"). Ambidextrous signified practically that one was able to use the left hand as well as the right.

Cinco de Marcho is bad Spanish that was coined by an alcoholic. It supposedly means "The Fifth of the Month of March," a punning reference to Cinco de Mayo celebrations in Mexico, on which, every fifth of May, our neighbors to the south commemorate as a drinking holiday a 1862 Mexican army victory over French forces at the Battle of Puebla. Was it an important military victory? Uh, not really. Cinco de Marcho, on the other hand, is a very important excuse to wend toward the nearest cheap bar, put on a silly sombrero, and get "tequilated" and end the evening with both your eyes looking like Dos Equis, that is, XX. *Borracho!*

Other unheralded holidays made up by students include Cinco de Drinko and Cinco de Gringo, often celebrated nightly among L.A. white dopers—never mind the damn date!

Retrolution

This inventive new word is a contraction of retro-revolution, a conservative distaste for anything new felt by elderly right-wingers. These dozing dinosaurs of dorkitude yearn to be living in some idealized American past—not the good old days of yore, but the good old haze of yore, where faulty memory and sclerotic arteries make them forget the horrors of the Bush past.

The Tea Party movement is retrolutionary, not very well educated, confused by modern life. They get their hearts pumping every morning by whispering to themselves, with the help of rabble-rousers and dumbagogues like Rush Limbaugh, "Who can I hate today?" The answers they come up with are: Hate everyone successful, hate all young people, hate minorities, hate anybody espousing new political agendas, hate everyone who does not do exactly what you and Lulu Mae do in bed. What do they seek? They fester in malice, hostility to everything, where, like sour cattle, they can bring up and rechew forever the bitter cud of bile.

Scrotund

Whoever coined the neology *scrotund* is a dab hand at blends. A chiefly humorous new adjective, scrotund means "having plump testicles and a capacious sac to hold them." The scrotum is the tegumental pouch that encloses the testicles and epididymus, and holds them outside the body because the testes require a temperature slightly lower than human body temperature to produce healthy spermatozoa.

Scrotum is one of many anatomical names that began as a Roman soldier's rough joke. Every archer in the Roman army had a leather *scrautum*, a quiver to hold his arrows. Thus this soldier's joke actually has a bit of poetry in it. The most familiar use of the word in English literature occurs in the novel *Ulysses* by James Joyce, where the hero Stephen Daedalus is walking on the beach and thinking of "the scrotum-tightening sea." Certain muscles contract when bathing or swimming in cold water to try to maintain the preferred exterior temperature of the testes by pulling the scrotum tighter to the body. It's amazing how many men who experience it daily can't even name the cremasteric reflex.

This cremasteric reflex happens when men are very cold, during the fight-or-flight response to shock, fear or severe stress, and just prior to orgasm. It acts to keep the testes warm, to protect them from injury, and to increase the propulsive force of seminal emission by decreasing the distance the ejaculate must travel during orgasm. The reflex can also be produced by stroking the inside part of a man's thigh in a downward direction. The normal response in males is a contraction of the cremasteric muscle that pulls up the scrotum and testis on the side stroked.

That's the Way the Pickle Squirts

One of the ways speakers inject verve and brio into everyday palaver is to coin new phrases based, not on changing words, but on inserting new words into familiar sentence rhythms of past sayings. This pickle saying may make preteen boys giggle furiously if they think it refers to ejaculatory trajectories, when in fact it is just a refreshment of "that's the way the cookie crumbles."

Myriad are the rhythmic variants of this productive oldie:

- That's the way the ball bounces.
- That's the way the cards are stacked.
- That's the way the stomach rumbles.
- That's the way the story goes.
- That's the way the bee bumbles.
- That's the way the needle pricks.
- That's the way the wind blows.
- That's the way the glue sticks.

- That's the way the apple falls.
- That's the way the pan flashes.
- That's the way the market crashes.
- That's the way the Cheney waterboards.
- That's the way the whip lashes.
- That's the way the gravy stains.
- That's the way the acid rains.

An interesting note about this expression appears in J. L. Dillard's *American Talk* in which he suggests the trope may go back to the days of frowsy mountain men trapping beavers in the Great Northwest. Sometimes beavers swam away with the very trap set out to catch them. Trappers attached a float stick that detached when the beaver made off with the trap and clearly showed the beaver had won that round. From this there arose early in the nineteenth century an expression among trappers "that's the way the stick floats," which was, claims Dillard, one of the earliest appearances of a sentence with this rhythm in English print.

Whornament

This is bodily ornament worn by a whore, bimbo's bling, jezebel's jewelry. You've heard of costume jewelry? This is washroom jewelry. This is a teeny purple cubic zirconium music box worn on a necklace that features a switch shaped like an erect penis. When ladies flick the dick switch, it plays "Feelings." Don't laugh. I saw one in Vegas. I heard it play. And the raspberry-vodka-soaked floozy wearing it? A guy could have caught the clap from mailing that lady a letter. What was I, reverent student of world languages, doing in Vegas? Why, you wound me to my pious core! I was completing fieldwork for my linguistic study, "Adolescent Table Dancers and Their Exotic Vocabulary." Whornament has also been suggested as a piquant synonym for "trophy wife" or "gorgeous but classy hooker dated just for this one evening to impress my fellow salesmen."

Zup?

All that remains of "What's up?" Nitpickers who find "Zup?" to be a shocking reduction should remember a far more frequent contraction that, in its introductory day, shocked British hearers: "Goodbye!" Why, it was considered sacrilegious to shorten "God be with you" to goodbye and even worse to "g'bye" and then—O mercy to a sinner—even shorter to "bye" or the absolutely heathen reduplicative excesses of "bye-bye" when God's name is completely removed from the farewell. A profanation of all that is holy! One contraction that has disappeared from spoken English is the Shakespearean cry of surprise or outrage "Zounds!" for "God's wounds."

Some of the words in language study that describe the spoken omission of various letters and syllables are explained below.

- Syncope is the loss of letters or syllables in the middle of a word, for example in certain old nautical words such as gun'l for gunwales or fo'c'sle for forecastle.
- Apocope is the loss of letters at the beginning of a word, such as lone for alone or round for around.

- Contraction is well defined by *Webster's Third New Dictionary, Unabridged* as "a shortening of a word, syllable, or word group by omission of one or more sounds or letters or by the reduction of two or more vowels or syllables to one—used especially of shortening in the interior of a word (as e'er for ever) and of shortening of enclitics (as 'll for will in they'll) and proclitics (as 't for it in 't is)."

- An enclitic is a word part treated in pronunciation as forming a part of the preceding word, such as English thee in prithee and not in cannot.

- A proclitic is an unstressed word part that depends for its accent on the next word, such as the poetic 'Twere ever thus for "it were ever thus" or 'Tis all I can do to hold my tongue" for "It is all I can . . . ."

Hold my tongue? What an apt idea! I'll do it. Until you turn the page.

Chapter 6

Every Night Is
New Year's Eve!

Champagne's effervescent history as a word and a beverage is here. I also toss in, as lagniappe, a modestly obscure word upon which to place a small wager at a New Year's Eve party. You bet the cultural know-it-all at the party that there is one word associated with New Year's Eve toasting that he/she cannot define and then bring forth the term *sabrage*. As you count your winnings, boodle not in mortal ken, you might even offer, to yourself, a toast. The word toast, too, is of tantalizing ancestry. You have probably been quite veisalgic once or twice during your drinking life and perhaps did not even know it! After reading this chapter, you will know it.

A Sparkling Histoire of Champagne

Ah, champagne—cork-popped, amber-foamed elixir effused in glassy flute, soon sipped to be savored by lingual papillae. The spumous jig of fizz upon the tasting tongue, the golden-bubbled barm that, cresting *sub uvulu* upon the pendent margin of the palate, seems to whisper to your throat, "Tonsils, stand aside, for down this rosy gullet, spumescent wine shall flow, the straw-hued ferment of a thousand suns."

The ever-effervescent champers, nose-tickling and tastebud-delighting bubbly, takes its name from a province of eastern France, not too far from Paris. She of the little black dress, elfin gamin, rococo Coco Chanel herself said champagne delighted her only in two life modes—when she was in love and when she wasn't. The quaint anachronism of rigorous grammatical gender, so burdensome in French, decrees that the wine is masculine, *le champagne*, and the vine-nurturing yet poor loam of the province itself is feminine, *la Champagne*.

How Was the Province of Champagne Named?

The Roman general Marcus Vipsanius Agrippa (63–12 B.C.E.) won the Battle of Actium, defeating Mark Antony and keeping the aspy Cleopatra out of Roman hair. Agrippa is said to have built the first Roman military road that terminated at Durocortorum, now Reims, the principal town of a Gallic tribe named the Remi.

The Romans began the names that became in English Rheims or Reims, champagne headquarters of France and still capital city of Champagne. Roman army victualers and sutlers, legend claims, brought the first grapevines, bagged on donkeys, kept watered on the bumpy journey by slaves, provisioning outposts of the empire with rough Roman vines from Campania in Italy and planting the viniferous creepers in the perfect chalky substrates around Rheims where, after hundreds of years of hand-rubbed hybrids and bee-blessed crossings, the vines eventually blossomed forth with grapes that would enable the making of champagne. Yes, Rheims was a little too far north for regular French wines, but for champagne, *le terroir est parfait!*

By the sixth century we have a written record calling the area *Campania Remensis*, Latin "the countryside around Rheims." Roman officials and soldiers posted to the area were perhaps reminded, by the vineyards and fertility of Rheims, of their native Italy and the fertile plains of *Campania Felix* south of Rome. In Latin *campania* means "land of fields" from Latin *campus* "field" but with the implicit sensory addendum, the developed meaning, of "country abounding in fields, country that consists therefore of fertile, level plains."

Some translate the Latin adjective *felix* as "fortunate" so that *Campania Felix* might mean "Lucky Old Campania! Wah-hoo!" I'm afraid not. The root in *felix* is *fe, which suggests always fecundity, teeming uberousness. The developed meaning of lucky or fortunate comes later. You were lucky because you experienced fecundity: your fields groaned golden with grain; your cows calved; your ewes lambed; your wife was a multipara. The *fe root shows up in words like *fertile, female,* and *fetus.* Cats litter many kittens and so the Latin word for cat was *feles, felis.* Feles means literally "one who bears young."

Campania was *felix* to the Romans because, for hundreds of imperial years, in Campanian fields grew all the grain that became bread for the city of Rome, at least until the Roman capture of Egypt allowed the import of Nile-watered wheat.

The Romans applied the word *campania* to other European flatlands. For example, the central plain of Hungary, the *puszta*, dry grassland once teeming with cattle, was in postclassical Latin *Campania Pannonica*.

Brief History of the Bubbly Itself

Cloudy, nondescript red wine had been made in Champagne for more than a thousand years by the only oenologists of the time, monks who needed income from the wine to operate their monasteries. This first Champagne wine had no bubbles and no reputation except as the crudest *vin de table*. The first sparkling wine from Champagne did not appear until the turn of the eighteenth century. The French monk Dom Pierre Pérignon did not invent champagne, but he did introduce various production and bottling improvements. It is thought that he might have been the first to keep the cork from blowing its place during fermentation by means of a wire collar secured to the neck of the champagne bottle.

Thanks to clever vintners, very early in its bubbling career Rheims' champagne became associated with French royalty. For centuries, from Clovis onward, all French kings were crowned in the Cathedral of Rheims, about a hundred miles from Paris. It was the Westminster Abbey of France. Fleurs-de-lis stitched deftly into cloth-of-gold twinkled like stars upon royal shoulders. Stone cathedral aisles bore the light tred of milady's slippered velvet and the soft padding of pert-bowed and fey-buckled shoes made from French leather creamy as butter. Sundry postcoronational shenanigans included the new king's health toasted with goblets of Champagne's local wines. Other European potentates attending French coronations took news of champagne and samples back to their own baroque banquets and regal feastings. Later, as the French middle classes grew richer, they looked for visible symbols of wealth to flaunt and found that greed could be voluptuous, found one perk that could be swallowed—champagne.

DING-DONG CAMPANILE

Someone once asked me if the Italian word for bell tower, *campanile*, and its root *campana*, Italian for bell, are related to the words above. Well, according to ancient wordhounds they are. Isidore of Seville states that the first bell foundry in Italy was in the city of Nola in Campania, as was the first belfry in a church and the first bell cast and gonged. There is no proof of such claims.

What about the Word *Campaign*?

As early as the sixteenth century, Italian used *campagna* in the military sense of army operations in open country (where most pitched battles of European history took place). *Campagna* stemmed from Latin *Campania*. French probably borrowed this sense and form to give *campagne* "field of battle.'" Metaphorical extension of the word to describe a political field of battle as in "election campaign" came later in French and English, rising in frequency of use throughout the nineteenth century.

The *Oxford English Dictionary* has this useful note in its Second Edition, 1989. "The name arose in the earlier conditions of warfare, according to which an army remained in quarters (in towns, garrisons, fortresses, or camps) during the winter, and on the approach of summer issued forth into the open country (*nella campagna, dans la campagne*) or 'took the field,' until the close of the season again suspended active operations."

A Toast to Toasts!

When an old year is toast, let us toast the new year. Why do we use the English word *toast* with those two meanings and in other ways?

The earliest meaning in English appears in a cookbook around C.E. 1430: "and serve forth all that as tostes." Bread roasted over a fire to a golden-brown crispness, toast springs from a verb that was kicking around in Old French and probably in early English soon after the Norman Conquest in 1066. Old French *toster* "to roast" stemmed from late popular Latin *tostare* "to grill, to roast, to barbecue." *Tostare* harks back to a classical Latin verb *torrere* "to burn as the sun does, to dry out by means of heat." We get the hot English adjective *torrid* from the same root.

How did toast come to mean the person to whom good health is wished by means of a communal drink, the act of toasting itself and the verb describing such honoring?

Writer Hyde Flippo, in an Internet note on German toasts, writes this: "The Merriam-Webster dictionary says the word is derived 'from the use of toasted spiced bread to flavor the wine [during a toast], and the notion that the person honored also added flavor.' Other sources claim that the word is derived from the 18th century English custom of covering a glass of hot spiced wine with a slice of toast as it was passed around the table. Each person lifted the toast, took a sip of wine, said a few words, and passed the glass on. When the glass reached the person being toasted, the honoree got to eat the toast."

New American Slang Synonym

The newest American use stems from a much older Victorian English use of the word *toast*. "That dude is toast" means the person referred to is in deep trouble, is ruined, is finished. This use was made widely popular by the film *Ghostbusters* in which Dr. Venkman, played by Bill Murray, says, "This chick is toast."

Several morsels of Victorian slang account for the start of this modern American meaning. A Cockney villain might have said, " 'E was 'ad on toast, guv." He was had on toast, that is, he was swindled good and proper. If you had someone on toast, you ate him up; you had him where you wanted him: anxious, caught, and squirming.

TOASTS FROM AROUND THE WORLD
- **Arabic:** *Fi sahitak*
- **Belgian:** *Op uw gezonheid*
- **Brazilian:** *Saude*
- **Chinese:** *Kong chien*

- Dutch: *Proost*
- Egyptian: *Fee sihetuk*
- French: *À votre santé / Santé*
- German: *Prost*
- Greek: *Yia'sou*
- Hawaiian: *Hipahipa*
- Hebrew: *Le'chaim*
- Irish Gaelic: *Sláinte* (pronounced "slawn-che")
- Italian: *Salute / Cin cin*
- Japanese: *Kampai*
- Portuguese: *Saúde*
- Russian: *Vashe zdorovie*
- Spanish: *Salud*
- Swahili: *Afya / Vifijo*
- Swedish: *Skål*
- Thai: *Chook-die / Sawasdi*
- Zulu: *Oogy wawa*

After All That Booze, It's Curfew Time

The first curfew was an order to cover and thereby put out live fire. The word began in Anglo-French, the dialect eventually spoken by the Norman French who conquered England in C.E. 1066. Medieval towns and cities were built of wood. They were dry tinderboxes waiting to be consumed in careless fires that were often left burning all night.

Curfew in Anglo-French was *coeverfu*, that is "cover (the) fire" from *couvrir* "to cover" and *feu* "fire." The Old French may have been a loan-translation from medieval Latin which had two curfew words: *ignitegium* and *pyritegium*, from *tegere*, Latin "to cover" and *ignis* Latin "fire" and *pyr, pyros* Greek "fire."

Danger burned not only in the crackling hearth of domestic fires but also blacksmiths' forges in whose sooty laps hot coals glowed orange all night. At first a night watchman on his rounds would call the curfew at eight or nine o'clock, reminding taverners to douse their firesides, smiths to smother their flames, and citizens to put out open fires. Fires contained in metal pots would literally have the lid put on them and be "covered."

Bank Those Uppity *Flambeaux*, Sire!

Some medieval hamlets required only that open fires be banked, that is, covered high with fuel wood or coal, and pressed down so that the fire burned slowly throughout the night or smoldered gently. Banking a fire means you restrict in some manner the amount of oxygen getting to the flame. A useful Wikipedia note reads: "The usual procedure was at the sound of the curfew bell the burning logs were removed from the centre of the hearth of a warming fire and the hot ashes swept to the back and sides. The cold ashes were then raked back over the fire so as to cover it. The ashes would then keep smoldering giving warmth without a live fire going. The fire could easily be reignited the next morning by merely adding logs back on and allowing air to vent through the ashes."

Ding-Dongs for Ning-Nongs

By the thirteenth century in England, curfew was the ringing of a bell, sometimes from a curfew tower, enjoining citizens abroad and afoot in the night to clear the streets and go home. These curfews were for security, to keep the peace and safety of the town. After the curfew bell, foreigners were not allowed to carry arms. Of course, curfews are still imposed on citizens all around the world, to quell riot, to stop insurrections, to moderate attempted coups d'états, to keep student or citizen protests within governable bounds.

In 1068, the first Norman king, William I of England, passed the curfew bell law. It was imposed mainly against the Anglo-Saxon underclass, so freshly conquered by the French. Fires, it was claimed, could be used to summon rebel Anglo-Saxons to night meetings where conspiracies of taking England back from the Normans might be discussed. Anglo-Saxons thus heard the curfew bell as the death knell of their freedom to associate and of their very liberty as free Englishmen.

Shakespeare liked the word *curfew*, but he varied its timing.
In *Romeo and Juliet*, iv 4,
"Come, stir, stir, stir, the second cock hath crow'd,
The curfew bell hath rung, tis three o'clock."

In *The Tempest*, v. 1, Prospero says:
"You, whose pastime
Is to make midnight mushrooms, that rejoice
To hear the solemn curfew."

In *King Lear*, iii. 4, Edgar says:

"This is the foul fiend, Flibbertigibbet: he begins at curfew and walks to the first clock."

Bonfire and Balefire

Another medieval fire word that sometimes causes confusion about its origin is *bonfire*. It is not, as many self-appointed experts assure the unwary, a "good" fire from French *bon, bonne* "good." No. It was first a Celtic bone fire, in which animal bones were burnt to ward off evil spirits.

Bonfire should not be confused with the Wiccan *balefire*. The word appears several times in Old English poetry from around C.E. 1000, namely in the great Anglo-Saxon poem *Beowulf* as a large open-air fire or a blazing funeral pyre.

The form of the word itself, balefire, is probably a redundant doublet. *Bael* is an Old English word for great fire, mighty conflagration. But it was replaced in many Old and Middle English instances by the word *fire*. As the term *bale* died out of widespread use, the doublet *balefire* ensured that all would comprehend the word, especially in areas where bale was no longer understood as an independent word. Old English *bael* has cognates in the language spoken by the Vikings, Old Norse, where it is *bál* "funeral pyre" and in Sanskrit *bhalas* "lustre, firey glow."

CHAPTER 7

Creepy Words

English, like all languages, has a night side. Tracing the moist
spoor of the deformed goblin down an echoic corridor of horror is
always fun. A whole special, cobwebbed vocabulary of the ungodly
and the ungainly exists, to frighten the reader, to tingle the spine,
to summon by obscene reveille the undead. These bristly terms
reside not only in a catalogue of demons but also inside the technical goobledygook of medicine itself. In this chapter we'll name a
few things that hide under beds and also look at some of the ways
some doctors use big words to hide the truth from patients. However well we may come to know the vocabulary of dread, it is hoped
we all maintain attentive watch on night things. Or else we might
endure the fate of the heedless archaeologists in H. P. Lovecraft's
poem: "We cleared a path, but raced in mad retreat, when, from
below, we heard those clumping feet."

Guards, Screw That Pilliwinks On!

Pilliwinks sounds like a word that virginal maidens half-clad in gauzy raiment and skipping through fields of fragrant posies might coo to some flitting lark. But pilliwinks is a brutal cellmate of words such as whipping post, gallows, stretching ladder, knee screw, breast talon, heretic fork, iron lock jaw, collar of thorns, head press, barrel pillory, humiliation mask, the wheel, garrote, tongs, interrogator's chair, hanging cage, Judas scale, the rack, and executioner's axe.

The *Oxford English Dictionary* defines pilliwinks with blood-chilling concision: "an instrument of torture for squeezing the fingers, similar to a thumbscrew." The pilliwinks was a small vice, sometimes with interior sharp points, that punctured the skin of a victim's fingers before his fracturing metacarpals and contused phalanges were splintered and agonizingly crushed. Fingers and thumbs were stuffed into the vice and the screws were turned until the prisoner's fingers were a blood mush of pulped bone and flesh. Across centuries of such horrific compression, one hears still victims' screams.

Pilliwinks is one very obscure term whose origin has been lost in etymology's cluttered attic. Some researchers suggest an improbable connection with the periwinkle flower. They see pilliwinks as a regional variant of periwinkle. Wow, those regional peasants would have had to have been really blasted on dandelion wine to alter periwinkle to pilliwinks. What, then, is the semantic connection of periwinkle to an instrument of torture? They can't explain.

Pilliwinks' Use Throughout History

The earliest mention of this mean machine is in the year 1397
C.E. in the record of an imprisonment for a case that had come
before an Anglo-Norman Court of Chancery somewhere in post-
conquest England. Here's the citation in Anglo-Norman:

*"Johan Skypwyth… aresta le dit Johan Rouseby et lui enprisona
horriblement en soun hostiel a Nicole [Lincoln], et lui mist en ceppes
et mist sez mayns aderere soun dorse, et sur sez mayns vne paire de
pyrwykes."*

Translation: John Skipworth arrested the said John Rouseby
and slapped him into prison under horrible conditions at the Lin-
coln jail. He was bound with prison chains (ceppes), his hands
behind his back (dorse) and on his hands a pair of pilliwinks.

Also from fourteenth-century England is this Latin description
found in a cartulary at St. Edmund's monastery:

*"Ipsum . . . cum cordis ligaverunt & super pollices ipsius Roberti
quoddam instrumentum vocatum Pyrewinkes ita stricte et dure pos-
uerunt quod sanguis exivit de digitis illius."*

Translation: They had bound the man with ropes and over the
thumbs of this same Robert they had put a certain instrument
called a pilliwinks. [They screwed it on] so tightly and with such
force that blood shot out of his fingertips.

Two hundred years later, the spelling is more familiar: "Alaster
Grant, who was indicted for theft and robbery 3rd August 1632 . . .
was twice put to the torture, first in the boots, and next in the pil-
liewinks or pinniewinks."

By 1819, a bedraggled wretch in Sir Walter Scott's *Bride of Lammermoor* moans, "They prick us and they pine us, and they pit us on the pinnywinkles for witches."

SUFFER THE LITTLE CHILDREN?

Were wee tots and toddlers exempt from this horror? From a 1594 legal document: "The dochter being sevin yeir auld put in the pinnywinkis . . . ." Translation: "The daughter was seven years old and was put in the pinnywinkis." One historian of England's Tudor monarchy tells us that the doomed Anne Boleyn ordered the nurse who was looking after her own daughter Elizabeth (later to be Queen Elizabeth the First) to use a pilliwinks to help straighten her little daughter's fingers.

"Sizes to Fit All Prisoners, Milord."

The squeezing vices came in a pleasing variety. After all, the vice-making blacksmith did not want to put a poor torturer off his game by making him perform too many adjustments before the screaming started. Consequently, there existed a little pilliwinks for fingers, thumbs, and toes, as well as larger vise-screws that fit nicely around an elbow or a kneecap. Nothing did more to assist a prisoner's focus on the truth than his exploding kneecap, a paroxysmal implosion of smithereened cartilage, sliced nerves, and bone bits oozing marrow and now unneeded blood.

But only nasty Brits and "non-resident alien scum" used such devil's paraphernalia, right? Wouldn't that be comforting? If only American historical writings from the 1700s onward did not tell of slaves being thumbscrewed for such atrocities as "did eat of corn beyond his ration." In one slave memoir, *The Interesting Narrative of the Life of Olaudah Equiano*, the literate enslaved gentleman tells of seeing finger screws regularly used to fracture the hands and toes of slaves on a Virginia plantation.

From Creepy Drows and Slinky Selkies, Good Lord Protect Us!

In the English language, the catalogue of ghoulies and ghosties and long-leggedy beasties and things that go bump in the night is a short one, a scanty list indeed. Modern American storytelling, whether it be literary, televisual, or cinematic, throngs with the same tiresome cliché creepoids: far too many vampires (I mean, come on, Dracula, never mind my neck; bite my ass, fangman). If it is not the undead cluttering up the back lawn on barbeque night and fastidiously saying no to the garlic ribs, it's blue-skinned, brain-dead tree-huggers from the moon planet of Pandora, goody-two-toes humanoid leaf-lovers pining and moping in that soppy interstellar snoozefest, *Avatar*. As to the dreary barking of were-wolves baying at a cellophane moon in every other horror movie, one shrugs and says, "Oh, go find a kennel and a prosthetic dentist. And for god's sake, if you insist on rending flesh, use Listerine."

I propose to cast a glance into the past and summon back to slimy life two Scottish night critters, dark things that were old when Babylon was new, one definitely creepy and the other? Well, you shall be the judge of the selkie.

Drow

Consider that neglected sprite, the drow, an underground-dwelling Scottish elf. You know the type, a stingy thing who would charge you extra just to drown a Barbie doll in the mossy-bricked shaft of the old well out behind the barn. Still, say it aloud: drow, apt name for an imp. More commonly known as trow or trowe, your average drow is inclined to be stumpy, ugly, and nasty.

As drow or trow, the word is a gift of Viking invaders who harassed the outer Scottish islands as early as the end of the eighth century C.E. and left their Shetland and Orkney dialects of Old Norse to be spoken there for centuries. In the language of that Nordic hoard, now called Old Scandinavian, a *tro* was a "fancy" or a "supposition." By adding the common Indo-European diminutive suffix /l/ you get the more familiar fairy word, *troll*, literally "a little fanciful creature." The form shows up in the Swedish verb *trolla* 'to bewitch, to make a charm, to summon a little fancy or fairy.' In Old Scandinavian, or Old Norse as it used to be called, the word for witchcraft is *trolldomr* "trolldom."

Drows prefer to live in earth mounds and knolls on the Orkney and Shetland Islands off the chill coasts of Scotland. They dwell in what the locals call "trowie knows." If the listener can manage to get the oatmeal and haggis bits out of the locals' mouths, that is heard as "trow knolls." Drows are chiefly nocturnal, and cheapskates to boot. Your average drow, to save a few pence, will hitch a ride on a bat rather than fly by itself to an appointed place of devilment. Drows are big on kidnapping, especially young people who can play musical instruments. Do you think we could slip a brigade of drows backstage on the set of *American Idol*?

A compelling origin-theory for drows has been proposed by anthropologist and folklorist Joan Dey in her 1991 book *Out Skerries—an Island Community*, published by *The Shetland Times*. Ms. Dey suggests the Viking conquest sent the local, smaller, dark-haired Picts into hiding in caverns, dens, and dank grottoes. She writes, "many stories exist in Shetland of these strange people, smaller and darker than the tall, blond Vikings who, having been driven off their land into sea caves, emerged at night to steal from the new land owners."

Lately, drows have enjoyed a modest revival, because they feature as dark elves in the role-playing game *Dungeons & Dragons*. R. A. Salvatore has even written a series of fantasy novels titled *Legacy of the Drow*.

Selkie

In the Shetland Islands and in the Orkneys, a selkie is a fairy creature that lives as a seal but can put on human skin. One legend says selkies were once human, but were banished to the watery world of the ocean for sins committed on land. Nevertheless selkies are permitted ashore in human form to perform certain tasks. Male selkies could come on dry ground and woo and mate with human maidens. Their offspring had webbed hands and webbed toes. One sees here a folk explanation of human children born with modest interdigital membranes.

The selkie stories suggested to residents of nether isles that some horny fisherman must have done the "naughty-naughty" with a female seal. In the Orkney islands "the great seal, the grey seal, the crested seal and others, are called 'the selkie folk' because it is believed that their natural form is human, that they live in an underwater world . . . and put on seal-skins and the appearance of seals to enable them to pass through the waters from one region to another." So writes Katherine Briggs in *A Dictionary of Fairies* (Penguin, 1977). The word *selkie* is a diminutive form of Scots Gaelic *sealgh* "seal." The Old English word for seal *seolh* lacked the guttural, having descended directly from Old Teutonic *selhoz.

All the Scottish tellers of folk stories make clear that selkies are not mermaids or mermen. In some tales, mermaids assist selkies and vice versa. Unlike other merfolk, selkies can shed their seal-skins on the land and pass for humans, but usually with tragic consequences.

Coating the Doctor's Truth with a Glutinous Glop of Smarm

Whenever repulsive details, sensitive emotions, or complex feelings of pride lurk inside certain words, then those words are subject to euphemism, even in a hospital setting. The ultimate obscenity in American culture is not the f-word or the c-word or taxes. No, the word that must be hidden from children, from us, and from old people is: DEATH! Eek! We don't care to admit often that people expire, bite the dust, buy the farm. Are you nuts, bub? Find some other way to say it. And that's exactly what euphemism does. Euphemism takes the clear but harsh term death and replaces it with a softer, sentimental, unctuously religious stand-in word or phrase such as "resting in the arms of Jesus," or "passed over to the other side," or "joined the Choir Invisible," or "called by God to eternal rest," or "is no longer with us here below but has escaped this vale of tears."

Euphemism seeks always to cover up harsh fact with weasel words. But, instead of saying "Bert is forever with his blessed Lord," I might have said, "He's tits up and takin' a dirt nap. Bert is worm food, dead meat." The movie *The Godfather* has a vivid non-euphemism when the mafiosi unwrap the dead fish and one of the hoods correctly interrupts the symbol to mean, "Luca Brazzi. He sleeps with the fishes." *Toto morto*. Luca was fitted with cement shoes and is enjoying a permanent vacation at the bottom of the East River. That is the opposite of euphemism and there is a term to describe that word ploy too. Changing an original word or phrase into one far darker, far worse than the original is using a dysphemism.

EUPHEMISMOS

The ancient Greeks used the very word, *euphemismos*, from *eu* Greek "well" + *pheme* Greek "speaking, saying," but to them it had a more circumscribed semantic than today. Originally *euphemizein* meant "to substitute a lighter word in place of a taboo word." Only later did euphemism come to mean substituting pleasant for unpleasant words.

Often euphemism is total evasion of the meaning by using its exact opposite. Consider fertility center instead of the logical infertility center, and mental health center for mental illness center.

Why taste the truth when you can use language to coat the truth in a candied syrup of gooey similitude?

Your Author Dons the Dramatist's Cloak and Sneaks into the Operating Room

In this little excursus, we're going to look at medical euphemisms, the linguistic cover-ups we encounter in brushes with the exciting health care system of America. First, let's eavesdrop in a hospital corridor and listen to one guy leaning sadly on a wet mop, as his so-called friend comes up to him.

"Hey, Lard Ass, you just get fired as hospital janitor?"

"I did not. I was recently decruited."

"You weren't dumped like last year's mayonnaise?"

"No. In the current restructuring agendum, I was placed on permanent leave, a simple act of normal involuntary attrition."

"Come on. The suits in management kicked you into the trash can faster than you could blink."

"You're so crude. My occupational locule and operations parameters became furloughed and then obsolescent."

"So basically you're out sitting on your flabby butt on the cement curb?"

"If you must know, I am presently seeking 'hiration' within a paramedical sanitational surround not subject to facility rationalizations."

"Bullshit!"

"Well . . . yes."

Once begun, euphemism, like milk left out too long, curdles into clotted, unclear language full of semantic mucus that has but one function: to hide clear meaning.

Let's say you are just back from the hospital having had a hangnail removed one afternoon. As you peruse your hospital bill for $19,000, your eye cannot help falling on several euphemisms in the computerized bill printout. Among my favorite itemized hospital fees: "disposable nasal-abstersion system" which refers to the cost of one hospital-room box of Kleenex, and "glaciothermal therapy enclosed media" for two bags of ice. Common all over America is the infamous "oral administration fee," that's the charge for Ms. Tiffany Twinkleton, the nursing assistant ancillary co-adjunctive para-aide handler (aka nurse's stooge) who picks up the little paper cup and hands it to you so you can grasp and swallow one pill. Of course, if your chart presents a posological bounty ordering five pills per diem, why then that's five O.A.Fs each day of your sojourn.

It's necessary so that the corporate bandits who own the hospital can each buy that second Ferrari. This is euphemism used to enlarge and enhance very plain statements or facts, usually, as in hospital bills, so that thieves can charge you far more than ought to be legal.

The Synonyms of Sawbones

Never say "What's up, Doc?" when you may murmur pleasantly, "Which supervenient and adventitious phenomena await our attention?" As I hope to demonstrate, some medical euphemisms serve a humane purpose, whereas other bits of medical jargon are used only to bamboozle non-medical personnel.

The classic example of a medical euphemism is the adjective *idiopathic* and its concealing synonyms. When doctors don't know the cause of a symptom or a disease or a condition with which a patient has presented, the doctor's report often states solemnly: patient presented with idiopathic myopathy. That means that I, the patient, came in with muscle pain and the doctors didn't have clue one about its cause.

Another sneaky word beloved of doctors is the adjective *essential*. "Yeah, Billy Boy, it's what we term, in the higher realms of deep medical thought, an essential myopathy." Here the word *essential* is used in an older sense than the common meaning it has today. Essential here means "having the characteristics of an entity," that is, the disease was felt to exist by itself, perhaps without a cause. Only twenty years ago, you could still find on a chart "essential hypertension," meaning: yes, this guy has high blood pressure but we don't really know what is causing it, so we'll cover up our basic ignorance of the etiology (medical cause) and make it sound to the poor, ignorant patient as if we examining physicians are towers of inerrant wisdom, instead of humble mortals seeking new knowledge to end their abysmal fountain of unknowing. Now, of course, I may have expanded the meaning a trifle beyond what the word indicates, but you get my drift. Essential is a bullshit adjective and should no longer be used in medical notation.

Another whooper of an adjective still used is *cryptogenic*.

"Now, Mr. Crasselman, you have cryptogenic myopathy."

"Excuse me, doctor, my last name is Casselman."

"Certainly, Mr. Kselman. It is good that you sought a second opinion. The first physician who examined you stated that your myopathy was idiopathic. I think, with no word of a doubt, Mr. Crottelman, we can say, with a good deal of clinical certitude, that your myopathy is possibly cryptogenic, if not indeed essential."

"What does that mean, doctor?"

"That means a $270 consulting fee, Mr. Catsasselman."

"Thank you, doctor. What's left of my mind is now at rest."

Quite Mad? Quite.

The dells of delirium and the ferny, thicketed, wild valleys of dementia are localities ripe for euphemism. No one in the family wants to say that Momma is gaga. Not even psychiatrists. The international bible of lunacy is a fat tome nicknamed the DSM-IV, in long form *The Diagnostic and Statistical Manual of Mental Disorders*, published under the not-always-benign auspices of the American Psychiatric Association. Although this is not the place for a critical review of the volume's logical and medical excesses, let's just summarize the current criticism by saying that some readers and fellow physicians think the DSM is an attempt to pathologize every waking minute of modern life.

My brief observation is that one corrective badly needed in the book is a massive rewrite by persons capable of writing concise medical definitions. The DSM contains few. But it does have a plethora of euphemism. I'm only going to mention one that falls into our line of inquiry here. In one place are listed disorders that may be labeled "delirium of not otherwise specified etiology." Disturbances of "indeterminate etiology" are listed. (Translation: "Honestly, Mrs. Mellish, I haven't a clue why your husband has taken to spraying Glow-in-the-Dark douche into his various orifices.") Etiology means "the cause of disorders."

Erectile Dysfunction

Sex provides a veritable waterfall of medical euphemisms, because sex has made rosy many a maiden's cheek down through the eons. Once it was an embarrassed whisper of "impotence." No more. Too offensive, although the word *impotence* was at least more pleasant than saying "limp dick." But look what happens to euphemisms. They become widely used, and then the euphemism itself becomes offensive.

Consider the happy-smiley TV ads of dancing postmen who emerge from their homes, fully breakfasted and maritally blissed, doing complex Broadway choreography because they finally got to play "hide the sausage" with their 400-pound spouses. In these ads, even the term erectile dysfunction is now shunned. It's too nervous-making. Hearing it, guys cross their legs and feel all icky. Why, one can actually hear the word *erection* in it. Yikes! Instead a deep-voiced, testosterone-soaked "stud" announcer intones, in solemn bedroom basso, the acronym, "Yes, George solved his E.D."

I'm waiting for the day when a television advertisement depicts a large penis skin lying deflated on the studio floor like an empty hotdog. Then an angel sprays new, emollient, fuchsia-scented "Perk Up" all over the fallen weenie, a spritz of atomized micro-motes bringing divine turgidity to all in need. Suddenly up pops the penis and begins dancing and singing for joy. This Phallus at the Palace will be the ultimate in the evolution of sexual euphemism. The advertisers will not even have to mention E.D.

Cancer Jargon as Medical Euphemism

Suppose a bedridden person has just been told he has cancer. In the initial days of his adjustment to this fact, his attending physician may have to refer to the cancer and may judge the blunt word too unbearable to repeat in front of his patient. Years ago, a doctor could have used the word *carcinoma* as a euphemism and been reasonably sure most patients would not have known this synonym for cancer. That is not always true today, when public awareness of the major diseases and the vocabulary used to describe them has grown.

But medical jargon provides a long list of euphemistic alternatives. Doctors can and do refer to cancer as "the mitotic figure, a neoplasm, a neoplastic figure." If a cancer has spread to form new foci of disease distant from the original site, they might say "the mitotic incident has metastasized." But plenty of patients know and fear the word *metastasis*. So more obscure levels of technical language and circumlocution may have to be plumbed, as when a physician might refer to one specific cancer site as "a melanosarcomatous excrescence."

In general, however, obscure technical jargon is not necessary during doctor-patient interchanges. Even in medical literature, one seldom needs to call a black eye "a circumorbital hematoma." Naturally, that is not said to deny the legitimacy of specialized medical vocabulary items such as cholecystostomy. On the other hand, yes, there are compassionate reasons for employing euphemism now and then in the practice of medicine.

Compassionate euphemisms occur all the time. An intern working on a disturbed patient seriously injured in a car crash, dazed but still awake and fearful, may say to an assisting nurse "severe heme loss" with *heme* being short for blood, the Greek root being common in dozens of medical words including hematoma, hemoglobin, and hemostat. In some emergencies, medical jargon replaces plain English, with the jargon fired into the E.R. air like bullets from a machine gun.

Dangers of Euphemism

You have twelve little pseudo-mini-legs coming out of the back of your head, at the base of your skull, due to a genetic birth defect. The first impulse of euphemism is to put a fluttering fan in front of your defect by creating a melodious descriptor that hides the ugly truth. Therefore, you are not what the other kids called you in public school "Hey! Lobster Head!" No, no, no. You are "of limbed advantage," or, even more awkward to say, you are "advantageously limbed." Such weasel phrases are created to totally obscure what is evident. But the truth is that you are not "advantaged" in any way by having twelve teeny leglets protruding from the back of your head. What you are is a wriggling freak in desperate need of either high collars or, better, immediate con-

sultation with a surgeon deft at excising monstrous, supernumer-
ary limbs and digits.

Euphemisms as Jokes

Emergency room staffers make jokes. This funning does not
make them evildoers from the pit of Satan. If you think the medical
personnel who staff big-city emergency rooms in the middle of the
night don't need a moment or two of relieving humor, you are clueless. So here are a few nifties from the night ward.

PPP can be scribbled on a chart. It stands for piss-poor proto-
plasm. It means the dude on the gurney in the hallway, the drug-
stupified, sclerotic, cancer-ridden, eighty-two-year-old alcoholic with
a cirrhotic liver that could be used as a first base pad at the next Yan-
kees game is probably going to be DBD "dead by dawn." I maintain
that PPP isn't mean-spirited, but rather is a signal to be exceedingly
careful about the application of crisis medicine to this individual.

Sometimes medical euphemisms can be coined. One I like is
acute hyponicotinia "desperation to grab a cigarette and a quick
smoke." At a bar near a downtown hospital, an off-duty Florence
Nightingale was wearing a T-shirt that read "WFFS" "will fuck for
smoke."

Medical and nursing students like to make up definitions that
may be on the next exam. Question: What is Throckmorton's Sign?
Answer: In the unconscious male, the penis points to the injury.

A very useful exclamation amidst the green bustle of an over-
crowded E.R. is the loud cry "Code Brown!" It means somebody
has screwed up and there will be shit to pay.

A terminal or actually defunct person may have a playful note attached to one toe that reads DDD "definitely done dancing." Is this disrespectful of the departed loved one, an indignity to a corpse? Oh, grow up.

Some euphemisms mock the very creation of such obfuscatory bibble-babble, for example, when you hear an intern say, "Chief of Surgery incurred an anal-cranial inversion." Translation: "That guy's got his head up his ass on all my shifts."

As our final jest, consider the funeral director at the crematorium who refers to each loved one trundling down the conveyor belt in his or her casket as "a shake and bake." Is that a euphemism designed to cover up something unpleasant? It is.

Veisalgic? You're Hung Over, Pal

As the booze-befuddled bashes of midwinter whoop-ups abate into residual head throbbings, a fancy word for hangover may come in handy. Especially apt, should one have to resort to circumlocution when describing, for example, the state of Aunt Tiffany after five martinis. One hesitates to say, "Tiffy is squiffy, pissed as a newt, stiff as a fresh-boiled owl." Auntie's family will better appreciate some periphrastic evasion of a pseudo-medical hue, such as "My aunt is sufficiently veisalgic as to require a taxicab." When little Rodney pipes up, "You mean, require a hearse!" the wee lad may be chastised repeatedly with a large candy cane.

Whatever befalls, here's an English medical word new in the twenty-first century. Veisalgia is a hangover. The neology was coined in an article by Jeffrey G. Wiese, Michael G. Shlipak, and Warren S. Browner in the professional journal *Annals of Internal Medicine*, June 6, 2000, vol. 132, no. 11, pp. 897–902.

Seven years after its initial use, veisalgia is fairly widely used in popular medical websites and household medical advice books. It is not yet listed in the *Oxford English Dictionary* online and has met a modicum of resistance from academic doctors and journal editors, principally, I suspect, because the word is a hybrid, that is, not made from all Latin or all Greek word roots. These are the same fussbudgets who criticized the word *television* when it was coined early in the twentieth century, because it was half Greek and half Latin. The horror! The horror! *Tele* means "far" in Greek and *visio* Latin "seeing." One supposes those critics would have approved some tongue-torqueing monstrosity such as "distantovision."

Post Coitum

The authors who made this new medical term state that the first syllable of veisalgia derives from the Norwegian language where *kveis* is a term signifying the "uneasiness following debauchery." But *kveis*, say etymological purists, is not an apt component, because the word does not always mean "hangover." *Kveis* may denote Norwegian postcoital sadness (Isn't that endemic?), that glum sensory depletion following intercourse. It may be termed postcoital *tristesse*, based on the old Latin humorous maxim: *post coitum omne animal triste est, praeter mulierem gallumque* "after intercourse, every animal is sad except women and roosters." There is no extant evidence as to which ancient sage determined the veracity of the Latin statement, nor is there mention of an ancient Roman S.P.C.R. (Society for the Prevention of Cruelty to Roosters).

REAL NORWEGIANS GET TOEMMERMENN

Kveis is not the common Norwegian way of expressing "hangover." Much more colloquial and zesty are *toemmermenn*. If a good citizen of Norway has imbibed too much Linie Aquavit and is plastered to the gills and feeling no pain, he is said to have *toemmermenn* or "lumberjacks" pounding their axes on the tender dendrites and axons of his brain cells.

Because one of the neologists credited with veisalgia's creation is named Wiese, I'm wondering if the word was even seriously presented in the paper. Perhaps it was a mere verbal *jeu d'esprit*, a punnish trifle taken up and transformed by use into a serious synonym for hangover. Odder things have happened in word history.

One Flu over the Cuckoo's Nest

It appears in the medical catchphrase, "Symptomatically, influenza is myalgia." I once told a doctor that I had just suffered a bout of the flu. He looked doubtful and asked, "Did you have any muscle pain? Any sweats? Any chills?" I said no and described my symptoms. "You had a cold, an upper respiratory tract infection, but not influenza." Myalgia is muscle pain, from *mys, myos* Greek "muscle" + *algia* Greek "feeling pain."

The root appears in the word *analgesic* "a painkiller drug or remedy" from Greek *a-* "not" (sometimes called alpha privative because it negatizes the word it prefixes) + *n* (sometimes called "nu euphonic" an n-sound added to the interior of words to make the word elements sound together more easily) + *algesia* "feeling pain" (from earlier Greek algos "pain").

FOREIGN HANGOVERS

- Danish: *tømmermœnd, rest, levn*
- Dutch: *kater, ontnuchtering, overblijfsel, overlevering*
- French: *gueule de bois*
- German: *Kater*
- Italian: *postumi di sbornia*
- Portuguese: *ressaca* (f), *sobra* (f)
- Spanish: *resaca (después de una borrachera), remanente*
- Swedish: *baksmälla*.

If you take away from this chapter one lesson, couched I hope in delight, make it: renewed attention to euphemisms, especially political circumlocutions and weasel words from corporations. Distrust every statement issued by big government and big business, for they want you to loll, somnolent as a suckling babe after milk, in the mortal nest of uncaring that only slightly precedes oblivion.

CHAPTER 8

Blushing Words

This section comprises two words of high taboo and one of lesser opprobrium, namely that ancient Greek equivalent of a male fashion model, Narcissus, with his fascinating name and his repellent philosophy "I'm just too beautiful for man or woman. I'm the only one who gets meeeee!" Some of these taboo words are considered obscene. They may well be dirty words—to some. But they are not to me. They appear in my book because they are sexual words worthy of study. They are terms with a piquant history that tells us how what is obscene in one age of English may be quite innocent in an earlier or later age, for English is a living language and subject to the metamorphoses—political, social, and linguistic—that all living tongues undergo through time.

So, even if you wish to get all harumphy and bluster like a dowager who has dropped a licked lozenge down her embonpoint, don't slam the book shut and whisper "What filth!" Instead, quell the hysteria for a moment, be an adult for three minutes. Don't mutter "Male chauvinist dirty oink pig of a swine." Instead, try reading my fascinating lexical history of these naughty wordlets.

Fanny: A Blushing Word's Many Meanings

With some trepidation I once tiptoed into the fray of obscenity by writing an essay about the etymology of the c-word. Immediately I was besieged as a writer/pig of the lowest order. Oinking plaintively I sought to exit the pig barn but was set upon and driven back into the ordure-thick den reserved for males who have transgressed. I was saved from despairing about humankind by several messages from readers. For example, a person identifying herself only as P. Y. sent me this e-mail:

Dear Bill Casselman,

I have a niggling question & after reading your delightful & scholarly "A Blunt History of the Word Cunt," *I decided you're the best authority I know after Eric Partridge & you may be able to answer it.*

What are the origins of "fanny"? In my native U.S.A., "fanny" means the behind. But my English friend Suzie says in Britain it means "cunt." Partridge gives only "female pudendum." But any U.S. dictionary gives "behind." Now, in Lyon there's the legend of the woman named Fanny who lifted her skirts & displayed her backside to be kissed by the winner of their game of "boules."

May I humbly suggest this as another area to be explored? I would be delighted to read another scholarly & picturesque bit of etymology!

All the best, sincerely,

P. Y.

To which I replied:

Fanny means "ass" or "bum" in American English. But in England it is a synonym for "cunt." But fanny is not quite as crude as the c-word in North America. British men use the c-word far more than North American guys. Sodden yobbos on the way to a soccer match may even criticize affectionately fellow British males with "You forgot the marijuana? You silly cunt!"

But still today British persons of quality, for example, Her Divine Though Withered Altitude The Queen, would never stoop to utter the vulgarism "fanny." Quite, quite infra dig., don't you see? Vulgar the word fanny may well be, but it is not as wince-inducing as coy nursery euphemisms such as "mommy parts."

AN IRISH DELTA?

The word *fanny* in Ireland usually refers to country matters as well. Consider this gross, misogynistic Irish putdown of an unresponsive woman, where the metaphor is Egyptian but the substance and the invention is pure Irish male chauvinism: "Deirdre's fanny was tighter than a camel's arsehole in a sandstorm."

Surprising Real Meaning of the Title of a Famous Novel

The title of the first true erotic novel in English, *Fanny Hill*, by John Cleland (1748), contains a not-so-covert pun. By the way, the novel is couched in glorious English, by no means in the sluggish monosyllabic tedium of most modern masturbatory porn. I read it in college back in the 1960s, but, as a North American English speaker, made no connection between fanny and the front of the female body. Fanny Hill is well worth any word maven's perusal. At the time, the social aspects interested me more than the linguistic.

"Fanny Hill" was local British dialect for "cunt." The hill was what delicate anatomical nomenclature termed the mons Veneris, Latin "'the hill of Venus," the bumper pad of fat over the female pubic bone, said to act as milady's shock absorber during more than usually strenuous missionary intercourse. If I'd understood fanny to mean cunt, I'd have understood Cleland's use of hill. The mons Veneris saved ma'am from too much slam. Thank Goddess!

How Did a Given Name Acquire an Indelicate Extra Meaning?

Well, it is not rocket science, is it? Consider popular synonyms, both current and historical, for the word *penis*, especially terms such as dick and peter, both male given names. English slang gives affectionate first names to genitals. Thus the feminine name Fanny became, probably some time during the mid-eighteenth century, a replacement euphemism for vagina.

In France, Fanny is still an approved girl's name, devoid of unsavoury reference. Think of the French movie star, Fanny Ardent. Its modern French popularity stems from Fanny, the eponymous young heroine of Marcel Pagnol's (1895–1974) theater play *Fanny*, first produced in 1932.

Fanny, Fannie, and Phanie are probably affectionate nicknames and short forms for Stéphanie, feminine of Stephen, ultimately from *stephanos* Greek "wreath of victory." Other, less probable origins may include derivation as a diminutive of the English given name Frances (ultimately from Late Latin *francus* "freeman"). Support for this notion arises from the fact that Fanny is a common female name earlier in England than in France, being widely used by the middle of the eighteenth century. After 1910 Fanny disappeared almost overnight as a suitable name for an English girl. By that date its anatomical vulgarity of reference had seeped up from the alleyways of London to become widespread. Persons of pith and merit could not possibly name an innocent girl baby with a synonym for "cunt."

Bugger All?

A common British expression synonymous for "bugger all" is "Sweet Fanny Adams." Here is one explanation.

It begins with a gruesome murder of the kind gleefully reported by the cheaper British newspapers. A young damsel named Fanny Adams was killed, chopped into little pieces and strewn about local fields and ditches in the town of Alton in Hampshire. A few years later the British Navy introduced new rations for its sailors, namely tins of cooked mutton. Navy seamen did not like the new rations and put about the rumor that parts of Fanny Adams had been discovered at the Royal Navy Victualing Yard in Deptford, a place that contained a bakery, vast kitchens and an abbatoir. "Fanny Adams" appeared in British slang to mean mutton or cheap stew and then anything worthless. The phrase "Sweet Fanny Adams" meant first "bugger-all" but nowadays as "Sweet F.A." is short for sweet fuck-all. And so, pious pilgrims of the word, we come to the place to put an end to all this fanny talk.

"Breaking Wind" Gets a Break

English contains a vast, vulgar, tooting traffic jam of synonyms for farting and for the verb, to fart. By the hundreds exist fart synonyms such as: anal volcano, bottom burp, let 'er rip, to poot (a supposed upper-class euphemism for fart heard in born-again nursery talk in the American southland), and a luff (a modest fart emitted while sailing). This tasteless abundance (or is it *abumdance*?) of flatulent equivalents arises from the preference of low-born louts met upon the common way to delight in obscene bodily reference, whereas persons of pith and merit, such as our fine selves, find such frolic utterly beneath contempt, *n'est-ce pas*?

I propose to begin with the coining of two needed medical words, sober scientific terms missing in the vocabulary of modern physiology. Never mind just breaking wind. We must give wind a break too.

Catapordosis

We have no serious word in English that means "farting excessively loud." Although the sensitive wayfarer encounters loud, inconsiderate farting at every turn of modern life, until now there has been no technical term for these vaporous audacities. I, therefore, here propose the new word *catapordosis*, of pure and serene classical Greek provenance, stemming from an actual Greek verb *katoperdomai* "to fart excessively loud" or "to fart at someone as a sign of contempt." The Greek verbal prefix and preposition *kata* has many hues of meaning. But one of its uses in ancient Greek was to make emphatic the action expressed by the noun or verb to which it was prefixed. Thus ancient Greek *perdomai* meant "I fart," whereas *kataperdomai* could mean "I fart excessively loud."

Polypordosis

Farting excessively frequently should also have its own medical term and for that anal audio show, I propose the new word: *polypordosis*, from *poly* Greek "many" + *porde* Greek "fart" + *-osis* common suffix referring to "a medical condition." Their proper accompanying medical adjectives would be catapordotic and polypordotic.

The Etymology of Fart

Porde is the classical Greek word for fart. It is cognate with all the Indo-European fart verbs, with Greek *perdomai*, Latin *pēdĕre*, Sanskrit *pardate*, Russian *perdet'*, and Polish *pierdzieć*.

Interestingly, our oldest Proto-Indo-European ancestors, speaking perhaps 40,000 years ago, had different verb forms to distinguish loud flatulence from softly, modestly emitted flatulence. We're not talking here about a squeezed-buttock repressed fart, but just about politely attempting to not break the chair in two every time you toot off. The PIE verbal root had two forms: *perd "to fart loudly" and *pezd "to fart softly." Lithuanian, for example, takes its fart word *bezd* from the second stem.

Bearing in mind the alterations that occur obedient to Grimm's Law, PIE /p/ becomes /f/ in Germanic languages and /d/ becomes /t/. So PIE *perd becomes *fert and *furtz, giving us Germanic forms such as Old High German *ferzan* "to fart" and modern German *furzen* and its noun *Furz*.

The Latin verb *pedere*, as might be expected, gives rise to all the Romance forms. Consider French *péter* and the noun *pet*. In Catalan, the verb is *petarse*. The Spanish noun is *pedo* and the verbs are *peerse* and *pedorrear*. The Italian noun is *peto* and Portuguese has *peido* and *peidarse*.

From the PIE soft fart root *pezd, Latin even had a word for an S.B.D., a silent-but-deadly or noiseless fart, *fesiculatio*, akin to the rare English fart words *fise*, *fist*, and *fizzle*. The original verbal meaning of *fizzle* was: to break wind lightly or silently. By the way, look up the origin of the word *feisty*.

Warning! Petomania!

A surprising English word is found in the now obsolete cliché "hoist with his own petard," made familiar to literate persons from its use by William Shakespeare in Act IV of *Hamlet*: "For tis the sport to haue the enginer Hoist with his owne petar." It means literally "blown up by his own bomb," that is, destroyed by his own actions. A petard was an early explosive device whose noise was likened to the sound of a long fart. Perhaps it took its name from the protracted fizzle of a burning fuse.

Briefly in Elizabethan times, English used the French word for fart, *pet*. Petard in older French meant "farter" or "thing that farted." English also has the words *petomania* (literally fart-madness) for a performance of musical farting, and *petomane* to name the odorous performer, after Le Pétomane, a French vaudeville performer active in the early twentieth century who could fart out simple musical tunes. And you thought Circle du Soleil was innovative!

Pēdere was the Latin verb for farting. The noise made by escaping flatulence, the fart itself, was usually called in classical Latin *crepitus*, literally "a noise" or "a creak." During the years when the very word *fart* could not appear in polite English print, a Latin euphemistic periphrasis was often used, namely, *crepitus ventris* "a noise of the stomach."

The Denial Couple

That kind of silly evasion of human bodily sounds reminds me of my stay at an upper-middle-class house with a married couple, severely repressed persons whom I shall refer to as the fart-deniers. If one of them farted at table, the flatulation could NEVER be mentioned, even in relieving jest. As it happened, the husband was catapordotic. He let the loudest blasts of flatulence I ever heard. But, though his flatus might unweave cotton garments, loosen flocked wallpaper or deafen household pets, his farts could never be referenced.

So one is dining in their home of an evening; crystal flutes of the finest champagne adorn each place setting when the husband abruptly fires off an epic blast of flatulence. It is a fart that shatters a nearby Royal Doulton figurine, a truly exquisite piece depicting some essential act of Englishness, let's say, a sportive corgi buggering the Queen. (Well, Prince Phillip can't be *everywhere*.) Suddenly the wife's face goes blank. As rare Spode teacups shelved atop the oaken wainscotting explode under the force of hubbie's bombardments, his wife Blankita murmurs, "My, the lilacs did well this spring."

Pfumpf! Spppfffertz! Ka-boom! Through his doubtlessly abraded sphincter, another anal cannonade volleys across their dining room, this time knocking the urn with grandmother's ashes off the mantel. A veritable mistress of the irrelevant obscuring remark, Blankita outdoes herself and says, "We think our parrot may be a crossdresser." I long to say, "The parrot won't get a chance to cross-dress if he is gassed to death, will he?" But, tame guest and stern guard of propriety's commandments, I repose in polite silence.

So, today, I ask you to remember and to use catapordosis "farting excessively loud" and polypordosis "farting frequently." Should you choose to neglect these brave new words, this entire essay will not be worth a fart-hing.

Queef: O Vulgar Verb! O Naughty Noun!

In North American English, a queef is air expelled from the vagina. The term *fanny fart* is commonly used in Britain and Australia. An

American synonym is pussy fart. To queef is to emit such air from the vagina.

Queef is Scottish slang, a pronunciation variant of quiff, meaning "vulva" or "vagina." This, together with British nautical slang where a queef is also a dialectic variant of quiff meaning "a blast of wind," combined sometime during the last 200 years in vulgar street talk to give the current meaning of queef: an expulsion of air from the vulva during or often just after vigorous intercourse, commonly called a pussy fart.

Quiff also meant a prostitute, and quiff once meant a puff of tobacco smoke blown ostentatiously from the mouth.

Another use of the form *quiff* is derived from coif and means a prominent lock of hair. This meaning is elaborated in vulgar American slang so that quiff means a girl or female, a reference to a woman's pubic hair. Slang of similar metaphoric origin offers the term *wool* as a street synonym for "sexually available woman." Wool is female pubic hair. By mistake, two straight guys stumble into a gay nightclub: "Let's blow this popstand before it blows us. No wool here."

Vulval Tromboning

Females may also induce queefs by bizarre bodily contortions or even as demonstrated in certain porno films, by blowing air up their vaginas. However, let it be known that blowing air into the vagina on purpose could cause an air embolism. In other words, don't try it at home!

A queef is not, of course, flatulence, so technically it is not a fart either. It is air, not waste gases produced by digestion, so often there is no attendant odor. It is a flatulent-sounding explosion of air from the vagina, caused by the pumping of air into it with a penis, or the spasming the vagina can go through during oral sex, gulping in and eventually expelling air. A great deal of vaginal air expulsion may cause modest vibrations of the labia minora, which, if audible, may create a sound resembling a fart.

So Why Is Queef Not in Modern Dictionaries?
Lexicological Fascism

Victorian prudery still rules among the skittish scholars in charge of admitting new words to the august precincts of the *Oxford English Dictionary* and the *Merriam-Webster*. Any word for a pussy fart must by its very nature be "dirty," spoken and used only by the lowest, most degenerate orders of society. In the case of the word queef, that is not true. Queef is widely used by North American English speakers under the age of thirty. Queef may never stain the lily pages of the OED because it is distasteful slang of the most transient nature, and soon, like much slang, will be mercifully absent from popular speech. Not true. There is good evidence the term *queef* has been spoken for 100 years or more. It's not new; it's not transitory. Queef belongs in dictionaries.

It is not the business of word-recording dictionaries to make moral pronouncements about words. That is the business of living word users, namely, our business. To not include vulgar spoken and written words of a language lessens the usefulness of dictionaries that brag of their comprehensiveness. Such censorshop makes their readers suspicious of what other words the dictionary scholars have decided are not suitable for us peasants to know. These namby-pamby exclusions are outrageous lexicological fascism, unacceptable in any scholarly venue such as dictionary making!

CHAPTER 9

Political and Religious Words

Oops! Here are the two topics one is enjoined never to discuss. The election and inauguration of President Obama were some of my happiest hours. The joy inspired me to wonder about the word *inauguration*. You can read my discoveries following, but the roots of the word take us back to ancient Roman religion and some very funny sacred chickens. In the history of the word inauguration, politics and religion mix in a glutinous stew of human folly and silliness. As a wise man once said, they are poor things, but they are our own.

The word *police* actually stems from the same root as the word *politics*; both are derived from the Greek word for city, suggesting that perhaps humankind had no need for uniformed guards until well after we threw down seeds by the door of the hut to invent agriculture and thus planted the germ of civilization, towns, and cities. You'll find the fascist fathoms of police word lore very arresting.

But most alluring are the roots of the word "god." To see how another language handled the naming of a supreme being, we'll trace the sources of Latin *deus* "god" and find that languages are always ready and willing to put names on the thought police.

Police and Polis

Yes, our word *police* derives ultimately from *polis*, the archaic Greek word for "big town." The Greek places so denoted were small as cities go today. We'd call them towns. Even in classical Greek *polis* meant not the city of streets and buildings, but the citizens of the town as a political group and their administration of their town and surrounding countryside. Polis also included many of the procedures and social structures necessary to operate the town and some of the countryside around the town, often called in English-written histories of Greece a city state, itself probably a loan-translation of a German scholarly term *Stadtstaat*.

Polis, as a Greek word from a Proto-Indo-European (PIE) root, is derived from and related to PIE roots such as *ple- and *pel- and their extensions *plen and *pler whose basic meanings are "full." Our English adjective *full* descends from the same PIE root *pel. Consider, too, one of its Latin reflexes, *plenus*, the Roman adjective meaning "full" in the words plenty and plenitude and plenary session. In the case of polis, its prime meaning was "a place full of many people," hence a quite sizeable town. From the same Indo-European root derives the Greek adjective *polys* and *poly* "many." In Greece during the sixth century B.C.E. such a polis may have comprised only a few hundred Greeks and a few thousand acres of nearby land.

When the Greeks referred to the city as a place of buildings and streets and temples and markets they used another ancient Greek word: *astu*, a word that does not have any common derivatives in modern English. But those who have read *The Odyssey* closely may remember Hector's son and that son's affectionate nickname, Astyanax. The people of Troy called the lad "prince of the city," because he was so like Hector, his beloved Trojan father, the boy's name being compounded of *astu* Greek "city, town" + *anax* Greek "lord" or "prince." *Astu* is likely to contain the Indo-European root *sta "stand, stay" and so its prime sense would have been "the place where we stay" as opposed to the many unnamed camps where as nomads we formerly pitched brief tents.

One of the first derivatives of polis in ancient Greek itself was *polites*, a word that meant "citizen of a city" from which sprang *politeia*, the abstract noun for citizenship. Then appeared the common Greek phrase *he politike episteme* "political knowledge," that is, the conduct of government. Our English word politics ultimately derives from such a Greek expression. We borrowed it directly from Medieval French *la politique*, which in turn had it from the Latin adjective *politicus*.

Here Come the Police

Late Latin used *politia* to mean "citizenship" and then "government" and then "administrative branch of government." Medieval French borrowed the word *policie* "political organization," from which English gets the word *policy*. A variant spelling in French was *police*. In C.E. 1687 a Roman Catholic theologian and writer named François Fénelon published a parental guidebook for the raising of pious daughters. In *L'Éducation des filles* appears the first printed use of the French word *police* in its modern meaning of a group of civil employees hired to enforce the law. About a hundred years later, the word *police* appears in English print with the same meaning. Another word, later adopted into English from the same Latin root, was *polity* "the form of political organization."

Here's a note on the early use of the term police from *The Oxford English Dictionary*: "The earliest use in this sense occurs in Marine Police, the name given to the force instituted c1798 (originally by private enterprise) to protect merchant shipping on the River Thames in the Port of London. The police force established for London in 1829 was for some time known as the New Police."

More Word Roots That are "Full" of It

The Latin word for "full" is *plenus*, the ancient Greek is *pleres*. Nowadays only a few learned technical terms in English theology use the Greek adjective. The word *pleroma* comes into English from Hellenistic Greek where it meant "fullness." In theology, *pleroma* is the fullness of God's being. *Plerophory* means literally "full assurance" and as a theological term it specifies "certainty about an article of Christian faith."

Polis is also related to a word in a fellow Indo-European language, Lithuanian, where *pilìs* means "citadel" or "castle," very much as acropolis meant in ancient Greek, the high (*akros* Greek), defensible part of a settlement. The Greek word *acropolis* is thus the "high town." Athens was not the only Greek city with an acropolis. Part of a nearby famous Greek city was called Acrocorinth. Sparta, too, had an acropolis.

Polis is cognate with the Sanskrit word for city, *pura*, which we still see in the names of many well-known localities of India and Southeast Asia. The common Indo-European /l/ for /r/ rule is operative here, where *polis* is one Greek reflex of the Indo-European root, and *-pur* and *-puram* are Sanskrit reflexes of the same root.

Indian Cities

Jodhpur is the second largest city in the Indian state of Rajasthan. It means "the city of Jodha," so named because it was founded in 1459 by a chief of the Rathore clan, Rao Jodha. Equestrians know a word derived from the name of this Indian city, *jodhpurs*, tight trousers used for horseback riding. A type of short riding boot is also called a jodhpur boot.

Singapore is the "city of lions" from Hindi *singha* "lion" + *-pur* "city." Although the island had many earlier names, it became Singa Pura during the thirteenth century C.E. when a Hindi-speaking prince named Malay Ammals mistook an island creature for a lion and called the island "lion city." Singa Pura eventually became Singapore. (Hindi is a language derived from Sanskrit.)

Consider the names of these other Indian cities. Mirzapur in northern India, home of Mirzapur carpets, is Persian for "city of the prince." Jaipur (Hindi "city of Jai"), the largest city in Rajasthan, was built in the eighteenth century by Sawai Jai Singh as India's first planned city. Dozens of other Indian cities have this root in their names including Ajjampura, Jabalpur, Kancheepuram, and Sitapur.

Sevastopol

This little harbor city in the Ukrainian playground of the Crimea is "city of the august one," named after Augusta Catherine the Second of Russia who founded the place in 1783.

The name derivation of Sevastopol works like this. The Greek translation of the Roman honorific for emperors, namely *Augustus*, was *sebastos* "venerable, revered, worshipped." The Russkies were being high-falutin' and wanted no mere Slavic name for this pretty little port about to be christened to pay homage to an empress. We need a Greek name, Boris. So, how about Sebastopolis? Then literally it will mean "Augusta's City." *Da!*

Chersonesos and Peninsula

Crossing the Black Sea, ancient Greek sailors had beached their ships upon Crimean shores and in the fifth century B.C.E., Greeks founded a port colony called Chersonesos, whose ruins may still be seen today in the western part of the city of Sevastopol. Chersonesos is the cute compound word that the Greeks used to mean "peninsula." It is made up of *chersos* Greek "dry land, as opposed to water"+ *nesos* Greek "island." So a peninsula to the ancient Greeks was a dryland island. Peninsula itself is Latin *paene* "almost" + *insula* "island." To the Romans, then, a peninsula was an "almost island."

NESOS, GREEK "ISLAND"

That Greek word for island lurks in many world place names today. Think of Indonesia, Micronesia "place of small islands," and Polynesia "place of many islands."

Other Polis Words

Annapolis, Maryland "Anne's City" was named in 1694 in honor of then British Princess Anne, later to become Queen Anne. Minneapolis, Minnesota is the "city of lakes" containing the Dakota word *minne* "lake" or "water" + *polis* Greek "city." The largest Minnesota city, it contains twenty-two natural lakes. The state's name is purer Dakotan. Minnesota means "sky-blue water." The fictional Princess Minnehaha, in "The Song of Hiawatha" poem (C.E. 1855), meant, according to the poet Henry Wadsworth Longfellow, "Laughing Water."

Polis (plural form *Poleis*) has literally thousands of derivatives in hundreds of languages, especially in the West, but also in the farthest-flung crannies of the earth. Metropolis had the first meaning of "mother city" from Greek *meter, metros* "mother." Metropolitan things belong to large cities.

Cosmopolitan is an adjective that meant, originally, a citizen of a cosmopolis, a "world" city from Greek *kosmos* "universe, planet." Nowadays the adjective cosmopolitan has such meanings as

- pertinent or common to the whole world: an issue of cosmopolitan import
- having constituent elements from all over the world or from many different parts of the world, such as the ancient and cosmopolitan societies of Syria and Egypt
- so sophisticated as to be at home in all parts of the world or conversant with many spheres of interest, as a cosmopolitan traveler
- growing or occurring in many parts of the world
- widely distributed

As a noun, a cosmopolitan is a person of the world, a cosmopolite.

A necropolis is a "city of the dead" or a graveyard, from Greek *nekros* "dead."

Istanbul and Constantinople

The root *polis* is obscured in the name of the once Greek, now Turkish city of Istanbul. The city's name sounds resolutely Turkish. But it's from a Greek phrase, *eis ten poli* "to the city." Say it quickly and shorten those Greek vowels, and soon you are saying *Istanbuli*. Now just remove the short /i/ and *voilà*—Istanbul. Note that the Greek stress is retained, even into English: is-tan-BUL.

The noun *poli* (now -bul) is stressed, not the preposition or the definite article—almost as if one were still saying the old Greek phrase.

Likewise, Constantinople was an earlier name for Istanbul, as was Byzantium. Constantinople is simply the city of Emperor Constantine, in Greek Konstantinopolis.

Naples and Nablus

Naples in Italy is another city named with a hidden or at least somewhat obscured polis. Originally a Greek colony and hence a new city, it was dubbed by the Greeks Neapolis "new city" and transformed by the Italian tongue to Napoli.

In the Palestinian West Bank of Israel lies the city of Nablus. By order of the Roman emperor Vespasian, the place was founded in C.E. 72 and named, in honor of himself, Flavia Neapolis "Flavius' new city" in Latin, the second word later shortened to Nablus. Vespasian's full name was Titus Flavius Vespasianus. Today Nablus' names are: Arabic Nablus and Hebrew Shechem. Hebrew uses the much older Jewish name for the town. Shechem predates the Roman settlement of Judea.

God and Deus: Two Words That Name a Deity

Whether one worships God, Zeus, Thor, Jupiter, or Giant Fruit Bats from the island of Mucho Guano, one may have mused about the origins of divine nomenclature. I don't mean the source of heavenly appellatives as explained in sacred texts or tediously elucidated from the implausible blatherings of holy writ. No, no, no.

Of course, the piety-blinded reader is free to believe tall tales from the ancient Near East. Gullible youngsters are force-fed daily, by televangelists of the lowest moral order, all manner of cock-and-bull fables. As a startled youth, I recall being appalled by the narrative excesses of biblical parables: the impertinent dead leaping from their shrouds in a brash manner ready to dance a hora, or a peaceful Judean hillside suddenly teeming with the outlandish replication of flat breads and bizarrely obtained fishes, transforming a simple landscape into some tawdry polychromatic extravaganza by Salvador Dali. What could be next, thought innocent I? A chorus of palm fronds singing "Thou art the Spring!" from Act Two of *Lohengrin*? Really! Was even a modicum of credibility permitted to invade these grotesque narratives?

So today those of us who would enjoy a brief respite from canonical hooey, in other words, thinking adults, we'll examine what linguistic science tells us about two divine names: God and Deus. We shall not pay heed to the gossip of angels.

Even atheists, however, must remember the words that poet Alexander Pope put into the mouth of Belinda's angelic guardian sylph:

"Know, then, unnumber'd Spirits round thee fly,
The light Militia of the lower sky."

God Changes Gender

God is the common Teutonic deity word, originally a neuter noun, *gudom* or *guthom*. The word preceded Christianity. The earliest

Teutons tapping a tom-tom at the toes of a tamarack, their privates painted with the blue dye, woad, would have called the Rootin' Teuton in the Sky *gud'm*. Vikings would have addressed their sky god Wotan as *gudh*. When the word began to be used to translate biblical Latin, Greek, and Hebrew into Germanic vernaculars, the neuter word God changed gender and became masculine, to match the grammatical gender of god words such as Latin *deus* and Greek *theos*. *He* is so much more comforting than *It*. "He is risen" may educe awe. "It is risen" could be the opening line of Dracula Gets a Hickey.

GOD OR gOD?

When should one capitalize the word god and when not? The *Oxford English Dictionary* has an answer elegant in its brevity: "When the word is applied to heathen deities disparagingly, it is now written with a small initial; when the point of view of the worshipper is to any extent adopted, a capital may be used."

The most ancient etymon of god is disputed. But it seems likely to have evolved from a form such as PIE *ghutom, a passive participle of a Proto-Indo-European root *gheu "to offer sacrifice to." Therefore the basic ancient meaning of god was "entity sacrificed to," an entirely reasonable meaning. The root is cognate with Sanskrit *huta* "sacrificed to."

Obscure Word of the Day: Theonymy

If you are among the word-hoarders who enjoy learning one new rare term per diem, here is our doozie for today: theonymy.

Pronounced: thee-AH-nuh-mee, it's what we're doing in this chapter: a study of the names of gods. An individual god name is a theonym, from *theos* Greek "god" + *onyma* Greek "name," pronounced: THEE-uh-nim. That's with a /th/ sound similar to three and thick, not similar to thee. When saying the words *three* and *thick* the English speaker sticks his or her tongue a little further out between the teeth than with the lighter /th/ sound in *thee*, which is made by tapping the tongue lightly at the back of the front teeth. Theonymy and theonym are words of an apparent obscurity so arcane that the two most authoritative dictionaries in English refuse to include the words. Yet they are recognized technical terms in academic theology.

Deus: The Latin Word for God

Deus is one of the oldest words in Latin, harking back to the chief sky god of the Proto-Indo-Europeans, one of whose linguistic descendants is Latin. The PIE word was something like *Dyeus or *Dyaus "light, daylight" and a related word *deiwos "a god." *Dyaus as a name word is related to other common Latin words including *dies* "day" and *deitas* "deity," a rather late Latin word coined from *dies* by Saint Augustine. The Greek sky god Zeus took his name from the same PIE root and so did the god who gave a divine name to one of the days of our English week. PIE *deiwos filters into Germanic as *Tiwas and Tiwas-taeg becomes *Tiusdage* and then Tuesday. Tiwas was the Teutonic god of war, just like Mars in Latin. That's why Tuesday is Tuesday in English, but Tuesday is *Mardi* in French (*mardi* < *Mars* Latin "god of war" + *dies* "day"). Tuesday/Mardi is "war god day."

Even *Dyeus phater, his longer PIE name, seems to have made it down through the centuries to Rome. The name means "daylight father" and changes several times in Latin, from *deus-pater "day-father" to *diupater to *Jupiter*. Greek had *Zeu pater* "Father Zeus." Note that PIE *dyeus phater made it all the way to Vedic in ancient India as *Dyaus Pitar* "father of the daylight." Ancient Indian Sanskrit had *Dyauspitah* and *Dyauspitrah*.

Deus Vult!

A stern Christian motto appearing frequently throughout the history of the Roman Catholic Church is the Latin phrase: *Deus vult* "God wills it." This was the battle cry of the First Crusade, said to have been shouted out by the crowd when Pope Urban II declared the pious march in C.E. 1095. This stark observation shows up on the signet rings of cardinals, and once upon a time was woven in golden thread on a pope's pallium, a shoulder mantle of white wool conferred by papal clout upon archbishops as a sign of office.

The phrase was also appended to the bottom page of the death warrants of innocent souls (children and women happily included) who were burned, drawn, quartered, disemboweled with their guts hung up on nearby trees in another cute little papal idea called The Inquisition. But it sure cleared those medieval roads of witches and made it easier for a 400-pound cardinal being carried by twenty crippled slaves to journey in a timely fashion along a Spanish road. You can understand how all those witches and their broomsticks could cause no end of congestion. French coats-of-arms and other heraldic bric-a-brac often feature the idea in French: *Dieu le veut*.

Opus Dei

The genitive case of *Deus*, that is *Dei* Latin "of God," is seen in phrases such as Opus Dei "the work of God," a controversial Roman Catholic organization. One of the Latin names of Jesus is *Agnus Dei* "lamb of God," also the name of part of the Roman Catholic mass. Some coins of the British Commonwealth bear these Latin words: Elizabeth II *Dei Gratia Regina* "Elizabeth the Second by the grace of God, Queen."

LIST OF PHRASES AND MOTTOES

Here is a brief sample of "Deus" phrases worth perusing. As may be imagined, the word is a familiar one in the mottoes of countries, states, institutions, and in the Latin liturgy and hymns of the Roman Catholic Church.

- *Te Deum*: One of the mighty Catholic hymns of thanksgiving opens with the Latin words.
- *Te Deum laudamus* "we sing our praise to Thee, O God."
- *ditat Deus*: "God enriches" is the motto of Arizona.
- *De Civitate Dei*: This is the title of St. Augustine's great early work *On The City of God*.
- *Dei sub numine viget*: "It flourishes under the will of God" is the motto of Princeton University.

- *Deo gratias* (D.G.): "Thanks be to God" can sometimes be seen on an ex-voto object offered in a church for some benefit or cure seen to be due to God's help.
- *Deo Optimo Maximo* (D.O.M.): "For God, the best and greatest" is even seen on old bottles of a well-known liqueur, Benedictine, because it is the motto of the religious order known as The Benedictines.
- *Deus vobiscum and Deus tecum*: "May God be with you." The first is plural, when wishing more than one person well; the second is singular.
- *in Deo speramus*: "In God we place our hope" is the motto of Brown University.

Deus Ex Machina

Nowadays a deus ex machina is something or someone who arrives at the last minute to solve what appeared to be an insoluble problem. Deus ex machina is in the vocabulary of any modern approach to the critical analysis of storytelling. In Latin it means "god from a crane," a direct Latin translation of a phrase from Greek tragedy *apo mekhanes theos*. Even the Greeks considered it a sleazy plot device.

The most famous use of the cheap, surprise ending is in Euripides' *Medea*. After Medea murders pretty well everyone in sight, all because her hubby Jason has cheated on her, Medea decides that a real grabber would be infanticide. So she murders the two little boys she had with Jason. When Jason rushes onstage to possibly kill her, Medea, by a miraculous divine intervention, suddenly appears high above the action in the chariot of the Sun God Helios, which carries her safely off to Athens and she thus escapes immediate punishment. When the play was produced in ancient Greece, the actor playing Medea was suspended from a crane. The sun is Helios, a Greek god. Thus her salvation was by a *deus ex machina*, god from a crane. A deus ex machina in later theatrical use could also mean a god who appeared through a trap door in the stage floor, such as a devil who snatched an about-to-be-killed villain and carried him away from death, but perhaps down to a living hell.

Sacred Chickens in Washington? Yikes!

Our question for today, political science students: What does examination of the guts of a sacred chicken have to do with a presidential inauguration? A spellbinding legacy of ancient Rome runs through modern English vocabulary, and nowhere more so than in the word *inaugurate*.

Inaugurate

In Latin, the prime meaning of the verb *inaugurare* (from the noun *augur*) was to observe the flight of sacred birds and thus determine whether the gods would smile on a venture either private or public, such as a new building or a national war. But the secondary and eventually more frequent meaning of *inaugurare* was "to perform publicly an official installation." Even to ancient Romans, the verb *inaugurare* meant to install someone into office after performing certain sacred rites of initiation. In Latin, *inaugurare* meant to deduce omens by watching sacred birds, hoping these portents would be favorable predictions of success.

Augury

Augury, performed by an augur, a Roman religious official much like a minor priest, did not foretell the future. The Romans believed augury displayed how the gods were disposed toward an undertaking—personal, governmental, or corporate. Would the new consul rule wisely and well? Augury would reveal an answer. But it would not predict if he would live through his consulship.

The augur predicted if the gods would favor an endeavour by watching pigeons fly off and interpreting their flight patterns, or by how sacred chickens pecked at their food, devouring individual grains of corn or millet seed.

Sometimes the sacred chicken was cut open and the augur gazed at its liver and other innards. Sometimes the freshly eviscerated entrails were cast upon holy fire (that is, tossed into a hot charcoal brazier set on a tripod directly beside the augur himself) and the smoke produced was "read" by the augur.

Romans didn't believe in augury with a deep religious conviction. In fact, the great Roman lawyer Cicero tells us directly in one of his choicest scrolls that he thought augury was drivel and nonsense. But, as to Roman religion, Cicero thought it was necessary for *profundum vulgum* "the lower orders of humankind" to believe a certain amount of mystical claptrap. It kept such losers quiescent and offered them pathetic scraps of hope that there might exist a post-mortem, post-Roman paradise into which they would be conveyed by Smiling Fate, perhaps astride gilt chariots drawn by winged horses, not as cringing, leprous underdogs with the IQs of dead gladiators, but as mighty Caesars, every trembling one of them.

AUGUR FROM *AUGERE*

I'm with the etymologist Fick who suggested that *augur* is from *augere*, a Latin verb that means "to increase, to promote (knowledge of something)." So the Latin agent noun *augur* is from an earlier *augor "one who increases our knowledge of the gods' by various means of divination."

However, the augurs had a union, the College of Augurs, which had real clout in ancient Rome. Unfavorable auspices (the prediction itself) could cause a major event to be postponed or canceled. In English, we still have both that noun and its adjective. We still say it was an auspicious occasion for the wedding. The sun shone. The bride glowed. The groom left his mistress at the motel and arrived on time. We still convene meetings under the auspices of (the good graces of, the empowering authority of, the patronage of) the mayor.

Etymology of the Word *Augur*

Augur might be a blend of two Latin words: *avis* "bird" + *garrire* "to chatter, to chirp, to blab." In this hypothetical and, to me, unlikely origin, the av- of *avis* must become /au/ and the gar becomes /gur/ to produce the Latin word augur. This is actually an etymology first proffered by ancient Roman authors. It is unlikely because there are very few other words in Latin, words whose roots are definitely known, that behave with such vowel-clipping and vowel-transforming starkness.

Auspex

But there is a reason ancient Roman word mavens were drawn to the "bird-chirp" origin of their word augur. A close synonym in Latin for augur was the word *auspex, auspicis*, an enunciatory contraction of an earlier form as in *avispex* "guy who watches the birds" = *avis* "bird" + *-spex* noun from *specere* "to look closely at, to observe, to behold."

We know that Latin verb *specere/-spicere* in these English derivatives:

- aspect
- circumspection
- in retrospect
- inspector
- introspective
- good prospects
- self-respect
- suspect and suspicion

The Latin plural of *auspex* is *auspices*. One Latin noun that was a synonym for *augurium* "the act of performing an augury" was the noun *auspicium*.

Haruspex

Sometimes a separate and distinct word was used for a diviner who only examined the entrails of sacrificed animals—not just chickens, but the livers of sheep, the galls of swine, the hearts of goats. He was called a haruspex from an Old Latin root *haru- that meant "guts" + -*spex* from the verb *specere* "to look closely at, to examine, to behold."

The Old Latin *haru- was cognate with a Greek root that we meet in English medical terms such as the phrase umbilical chord. The Greek cognate of Latin *haru- was χορδή chorde "a string of gut" or "the string of a lyre."

The Most Famous Roman Augury Not Performed

Recounted by many Roman writers throughout her history, this familiar anecdote was a cautionary tale passed on to make super-stitious Romans nervous about the petulance and mopery of their gods, for the less well-educated ancient Roman believed that the slightest infraction of divine writ would send Jupiter himself into a colossal and vindictive hissy-fit, from whose ill effects the trans-gressor might never recover.

The Roman general Publius Claudius Pulcher (died 249 B.C.E) was consul and commander of the Roman fleet fighting the navy of Carthage in the Mediterranean Sea during the first Punic War. Just before the Battle of Drepanum off the western coast of Sicily, like any good Roman general, Publius called for an augury to be performed, that he might see if the gods would favor Rome in this upcoming naval battle.

Suddenly on deck the augur tugged at his toga, cringed and bent low before the mighty general. Deeply embarrassed was the augur because the sacred chickens would not eat!

If the damn chickens did not peck at the grain tossed down on the deck of the general's ship, how would his soldiers and naval officers know if Neptune and his buddy-god Mars were smiling on them, if the sea god and the god of war would grant the Romans yet another crushing aquatic victory?

General Publius ordered his onboard augur to cast the corn niblets a second time upon the deck. A second time the frowsy chickens looked down their beaks at the corn kernels and refused to eat. They clucked stupidly and looked up at the augur holding his short lituus or diviner's rod. One chicken pecked at the augur's left toe. He was wearing sandals and the peck hurt.

Publius was nervous and full of rage. The Romans had little experience in naval warfare prior to the First Punic War, whereas the Phoenician or Punic navy from Carthage comprised the best sailors on the Mediterranean, oarsmen and coxswains with years of peacetime training in the rowing of Phoenician triremes (war ships with three levels of rowers propeling the ship).

Then General Publius squinted. Flashing mirrors from other Roman ships told in primitive signal code that Phoenician triremes now sped toward his Roman fleet. The sands of destiny spilled like dried Roman blood through an hourglass held high at the bow of the general's ship by the slave of the watch. Publius kicked the gunwales in growing rage. Still the sacred chickens did not eat one kernel. Screaming above the roar of the waves, General Publius ordered his augur to put the chickens back into their cages. Pale with dread, the augur did so.

Then, exasperated, Publius himself picked up one of the cages and tossed the scared and sacred chickens, cage by squawking cage, overboard, into the slate-grey billows of the Mediterranean. "If you little buggers don't want to eat, maybe you'd like to go for a swim?" yelled Publius.

What can I tell you, history lovers? Flapping flightless, useless wings, all the sacred chickens drowned.

Later that day Publius lost the sea battle of Drepanum. Unwisely had the general defied Fate and the ordained ceremonies of Jupiter and the gods. Immediately Publius was recalled to Rome and publicly humiliated as a loser. Soon afterward the hapless general committed suicide, a self-destruction brought on by fatal shame. From the long perspective of historical déjà-vu, one can only gaze backward in time and murmur thoughtfully, "I told you and I told you, Publius, don't fuckin' mess with the sacred chickens."

It does not matter that we today, reading the tale, realize the Romans loved this story because it blamed the gods and was exculpatory of Roman incompetence. Who knew the sacred chickens would go on a diet six minutes before a war started? Who could know? Auguries never revealed that kind of info. The anecdote conveniently omits the fact that the Romans did not know a damn thing about how to conduct a battle at sea. Rome however was a quick learner. Eventually Rome won the Punic wars and destroyed Carthage, fulfilling the order of Cato the Elder, a senator who years before had cried out repeatedly, *"Carthago delenda est!"* Carthage must be destroyed! And so it was. By Rome.

Like many words, inauguration has a history and has something to tell present-day users of English.

CHAPTER 10

A Modest Residuum of
Uncategorized Monographs

That's right; this is a grab bag, a hodgepodge, a ragbag, a verbal pawnshop where we display for your delectation and delight word stories that would not slip with ease into previous chapters. It's a miscellany of lexical legerdemain that highlights some of my own favorite bits of lore. From the lowest rank of sports reporting clichés to the many words for snow, you'll find the following a delightful mix. So, please, if you will snuffle and root here, I promise you will emerge with the occasional truffle.

The Sports Cliché "Hat Trick"

Where did the expression "hat trick" originate? The cricket term hat trick appeared first in British print in 1858. It refers to one player scoring three times in a row. In cricket jargon, one bowler takes three wickets with three balls in a row. That player was then permitted to pass around his hat and collect a few modest financial tributes to his finesse in the form of British pennies. So runs one hat trick story. Another says the cricket club bought the hat-tricking player a new hat.

In baseball a pitcher might strike out three batters in a row or a batter might score three home runs in one game. Three goals in one soccer game is also a hat trick. But the British sporting term was borrowed and became most popular in North American hockey. When a player scores three successive goals in a row, that's hockey's most impressive hat trick. A hat trick may also consist of three goals scored by one player any time in one game, even if other players score goals between the hat-tricker's goals. Today fans often toss their hats onto the ice or into the air to celebrate the achievement, although the price of monogrammed tractor caps is making even this modest whoop-up problematical.

The most famous such triple-scoring phenomenon in hockey happened in March of 1952. The New York Rangers were playing a home game, the last of the hockey season, against the Chicago Blackhawks. Both teams had been eliminated from playoff possibility. So the game was not crucial, and this prompted the Ranger coach to put in a rookie goaltender to guard the New York posts. Blackhawk right-winger Bill Mosienko (1921–1994) took superb advantage of the Rangers' neophyte net-minder. Mosienko slapped the puck into the net at six minutes and nine seconds into the third period. Then Mosienko scored again eleven seconds later! While the shell-shocked Ranger goalie was composing his explanatory letter home to Dad, guess what? Mosienko slammed puck rubber on net rope again with a third goal ten seconds after the second goal. A hat trick indeed. Three goals in twenty-one seconds!

Two Toronto origins are sometimes still presented in Canadian hockey histories. They are in fact only post-factum spin-offs. At Toronto's former temple of puckdom, Maple Leaf Gardens, anecdotal evidence says that a Toronto haberdasher presented a new hat to any player who scored three goals. It was also claimed that the Biltmore Hat Company, which sponsored the Guelph Biltmores of the Ontario Hockey League, began the free hat trick. No documentary evidence whatsoever supports a Canadian origin of the term hat trick.

Verbal Oddments and Tidbits

This time, we'll begin our look at some rare word broth by plucking from the cauldron of obscurity a gruesome technical term from Christian religious studies. I must confess here that it was obscure terms that kept my nose stuck in childhood dictionaries, kept me riffling through old yellow word books instead of being a manly North American little boy and learning how to fire a howitzer at the age of seven or abase myself in the torture of cub scout meetings. Now, after sixty years of collecting the disjecta membra of the body of our capacious English language, I can't think of a better use of childhood's amazingly efficient time of verbal acquisition.

Suppedaneum

A suppedaneum was a foot support for someone being crucified. Made of wood, it projected out from the upright, vertical stake

of the crucifix. The Italian painter Giotto often shows a suppedaneum as a detail in his paintings of the Crucifixion.

Suppedaneum is a Late Latin compound word from *sub* Latin
"under" + *pes, pedis* Latin "foot" + noun and adjectival suffix
"*-aneus, -anea, -aneum.*"

What Is a Glottal Stop? What Is Assimilation?

Why is the form *suppedaneum* with two /p/s instead of the more
logical form *subpedaneum? Because of a speaking process that
linguists call assimilation. When the prefix *sub* was put in front of
a Latin word root that began with m, r, c, f, g, or p, the /b/ in sub
usually changed into the first letter of the root word. This assimilation appears in Latin-derived English words such as *succeed, suffer, suggest, summon, suppose,* and *surrogate.*

In quick Latin speech, the /b/ in *sub* was influenced by the /p/
in front of it. Both sounds are plosives. This is exceedingly common in Latin compound words. It is far easier to turn the /b/ into a
/p/ than to try to pronounce both the /b/ and the /p/. In order to do
this, the speaker actually has to introduce a new consonant into the
word, namely a glottal stop. When a careful English speaker says
aloud and distinctly the words, "sub park," he or she must open
and close the glottis in order to produce two puffs of air to sound
both the /b/ and the /p/. That is a glottal stop or voiceless glottal
plosive.

In some dialects, a glottal stop actually replaces the letter.
Think of the British Cockney pronunciation of the word *bottle.*
One seldom hears a /t/ sound. Instead Cockney bottle sounds like

buh-ul. In some languages the glottal stop is actually a letter of the alphabet, for example, in Arabic. The International Phonetic Alphabet or IPA has a symbol to represent a glottal stop. Based on a letter in the Arabic alphabet representing one of the Arabic stops, the IPA glottal stop symbol looks like a question mark without its bottom dot.

Mentum

Mentum is the Latin and current international medical term for the human chin. Mentum "chin" has a rare adjective *mental*, which is sometimes confused with the adjective *mental* "pertaining to the mind" from Latin *mens, mentis* "mind."

No, the ancient Romans did not think the brain was located in the chin. A student of Latin forced to read the entire remnants of the incessant blatherings of old Rome's biggest blabbermouth, the lawyer Cicero, might however come to this conclusion. Cicero, a bloated pustule of arrogance, actually had a slave follow him about with a wax tablet to jot down every single thing Cicero said, just in case a Ciceronian felicity occurred.

But let me forget about ploughing through that tedious lawyer's yammerings, and return to *mentum*, a Latin word related to the Indo-European root that also gives us the common English word *mouth*. The *mentum* that signifies chin is not related to *mens, mentis* "mind."

Adjectivally speaking, there are two separate words spelled m-e-n-t-a-l. One refers to the mind, the other to the chin.

Mentoplasty is any cosmetic surgical procedure designed to change the shape of the chin to better match the rest of the patient's facial proportion. Genioplasty, a rarer term for the same procedure, uses the Greek word for chin instead of the Latin one. Γένειον (geneion) is the ancient Greek word for chin.

The Indo-European base whose Latin reflex was *mentum* "chin" also gives cognates such as modern German *Mund* "mouth" and Danish *mund* and Icelandic *munnur* "mouth." The Proto-Indo-European root has a prime meaning of "jut out, project over or threaten."

Orthoepist

An orthoepist is a linguist who specializes in the correct pronunciation of the sounds of a particular language. She or he is one who practices orthoepy—strict pronunciation.

Orthoepist = *orthos* "straight, correct, upright" + *epos* "word" + *-istes* common Greek agent noun suffix that means "one who [+ verb]."

In ancient Greek, *epos* also had a collective meaning of "narrative" or "chanted song." *Epikos*, its adjective, gives us both the English adjective *epic* and the noun *epic*. The two great epics of Greek literature are the *Iliad* and the *Odyssey*.

Membranous Labyrinth

In human anatomy, the membranous labyrinth is a network of three little ducts filled with fluid that hang down inside the semicircular canals of the inner ear. These ducts sway gently and touch one another as the human body and head move. Part of our sense of balance is created and fine-tuned as the membranous labyrinth sways.

Membrana is a tissue that covers a body part. *Labyrinthos* is Greek, "a maze," but the word was first applied to a maze under a royal palace on the island of Crete. So old is the word labyrinth that it is pre-Greek. It existed, perhaps in a pre-Greek "Pelasgian" language, before the Dorians invaded Greece bringing an early Hellenic horse culture with them.

Root 1: *Labrys*

A labrys was a kind of axe in ancient Greece and Egypt with two blades, so that the word *labyrinthos* means literally "the place of the double-axe."

Root 2: *-Inthos*

The second element in labyrinth is *-inthos*, a pre-Greek Pelasgian locative meaning "place of" seen in pre-Greek place names such as Corinth.

Incidentally, our currant, a dried fruit prepared from a seedless grape grown in the Levant, owes its name to Corinth. The chewy cookery ingredient was once, in Old French, *raisin de Corauntz*, "raisin of Corinth," corrupted to currant by the English, who could never speak French.

Ruins of a palace bearing emblems of the double-axe have been found at Knossos on Crete. Part of the legend of the Minotaur and its maze built by mythical Daedalus arose as folktales about this great palace.

The term *labyrinth* is often used interchangeably with maze, but modern scholars of the subject use a stricter definition. For them, a maze is a tour puzzle in the form of a complex branching passage with choices of path and direction. A single-path (or uni-cursal) labyrinth has only a single path to the center. A labyrinth has an unambiguous through-route to the center and back and is not designed to be difficult to navigate. This unicursal design was widespread in artistic depictions of the Minotaur's labyrinth, even though both logic and literary descriptions of it make it clear that the Minotaur was trapped in a multicursal maze.

Pogonotrophy

Pogonotrophy is the growing of a beard. It's a word borrowed directly from the writings of the Hellenistic Greek historian Plu-tarch, and is made up of two Greek components *pogon* "beard" + *trophia* "nourishment, growing, feeding." The literal meaning of muscular dystrophy means the muscles are not fed properly.

If a body part suffers atrophy, it withers because its cells are not fed (common Greek negative prefix *a-* + root).

Other words with *pogon* include the name of a genus of beauti-ful flowering perennials, *Ophiopogon* or snakesbeard. *Ophis* is one of the ancient Greek words for snake.

Mandrinette

Here's a plant name to try out on your know-it-all gardening friends. They won't know it. So make a bet, win the bet, and make a few dollars to put toward your purchase of spring seeds.

Mandrinette is a very rare, endangered hibiscus that grows in nature only on several mountains on the island of Mauritius and on a few neighboring isles.

Mauritius is an independent parliamentary democracy on islands in the Indian Ocean off the lower east coast of Africa, about 600 miles east of Madagascar.

Mandrinette's botanical binomial, *Hibiscus fragilis*, hints at the plant's tenuous earthly stand. Members of the hibiscus family may be labeled with the lovely adjective, malvaceous, drawn from the botanical name of the hibiscus family, Malvaceae, that is, the mallows.

I had the notion once that the Reverend Hibiscus Mallow would be an apt name for a repressed Anglican vicar in an English novel. At the novel's end, Reverend Mallow would be apprehended in the act of interfering in an untoward manner with a warm mince pie.

Mandrinette, a carmine-petaled beauty, is similar to Chinese hibiscus, *Hibiscus rosa-sinensis*, the most common hibiscus of worldwide commercial horticulture. The commercial plant was introduced by gardeners into Mauritius plantings and began to hybridize with the rarer native mandrinette to the point where the mandrinette could not reproduce a pure strain.

After mandrinette's approaching extinction was revealed, islanders successfully extirpated the invasive hibiscus. Today mandrinette seedlings are being grown at the Royal Botanic Gardens at Kew in England for reintroduction of the native island plant.

Shockingly, the now widely used English word mandrinette is *not* in the *Oxford English Dictionary* or the *Unabridged Merriam-Webster*.

Well . . . perhaps not widely used, but a wordlet of sufficient recognitory status to have drawn my humble attention.

Mandrinette may appear to be derived from mandarin, but it is a diminutive of the French medical word *mandrin*, a stylet, a slender wire put through a catheter to clear it or to keep it rigid to ensure the catheter's patency. Thus mandrinette means "little wire," a reference to slender flower parts of this hibiscus, perhaps to its elongated stamens.

Rongeur

A rongeur is a type of forceps with a gripping action used in surgery and dentistry. It is used to extract small pieces of bone during surgical repair or to remove osseous edges to enlarge a hole in a bone. A cystoscopic rongeur used to be employed frequently to break up the more friable gallstones. Side-cutting rongeurs used in oral surgery are called alveotomy shears.

Rongeur's literal meaning in French is "a gnawing, a chewer, a rodent." It is an agent noun from the French verb *ronger* "to gnaw, to eat away at." The French verb form *ronger* is influenced by two different Latin verbs: *rumigare* "to chew, to gnaw" and *rodere* "to gnaw." An animal that gnaws habitually is, of course, a rodent. Consider the metaphoric phrasal French verb *ronger son frein* "to be impatient," literally said of a horse "to chew on the reins."

French-speakers, like English-speakers, endure *l'habitude de se ronger les ongles* meaning "the habit of nail-biting."

A more idiomatic verbal phrase is *se ronger les sangs à propos de*, which means "to be worried sick about . . . ."

La Ronge, Saskatchewan, Canada

We even find *ronger* place-name derivatives on a map of Canada. One place name that hides its beavery origin is La Ronge, Saskatchewan, named after Lac La Ronge. In Alan Rayburn's excellent *Dictionary of Canadian Place Names* (Oxford University Press, 1997), Canada's prime toponymist states "it may have been named either because the jagged shoreline had the appearance of having been gnawed by Kitchi Amik, the Great Beaver, or because early voyageurs discovered trees along its shoreline gnawed by beavers."

La ronge in seventeenth-century French referred to food that appeared to have been gnawed by an animal. French-speaking voyageurs canoeing across what would become Canada used the noun to refer to beaver-chewed tree stumps.

Snow Job: Snow Words of Exquisite Rarity

What did the Alaskan prostitute give her customer? A snow job. What did the Chernobyl prostitute give her customer? A glow job. The most frequent snow job of unlettered pop word study is the often-repeated error that the Inuit people have sixty-nine words for snow. It's wrong because the many snow expressions in their languages, such as Inuktitut, are not technically words; many of them are sentences, due to the structure of such northern tongues. But all that is explained in other volumes of niveous trivia. My contention here is equally simple: English, not Inuktitut, may well have more than seventy terms for various forms of snow or snow-related entities.

In this piece, my purpose is to augment your hibernal word hoard, to acquaint you with some of the rarer, more exquisite garments lifted from winter's verbal trunk. And we'll ski off with the very word *winter*. Winter's root is wet, literally. The same Germanic root that gives us our words water and wet makes the first vowel nasal and so adds an *n*, thus *ued > *wet > *went > *wint > winter.

An alternate source for the word *winter* may stretch all the way back to a root form in Proto-Indo-European *ueid that gives Celtic words for "white"; compare, for example, Old Irish *find* "white" and many other Celtic cognates such as Welsh *gwyn* "white" and perhaps even the Druids "people of the white oak" from *dru-ueid or oak-white. Dru means "oak tree" and there are two PIE morphemes represented as *ueid.

The second *ueid means "know, see." One of its reflexes in English is the word *wit* with its prime meaning of insight. In Latin, PIE *ueid displays as *videre* "to see." Take *dru and *ueid compounded to make the word Druid, and the Druids could be the "oak-knowers" based on their veneration of the oak tree and its mistletoe.

In what may be Shakespeare's most felicitous outset, the bard put these opening lines into the mouth of King Richard the Third: "Now is the winter of our discontent/Made glorious summer by this son of Yorke."

The Victorian poet Alfred, Lord Tennyson, liked the gelid sound of the word too. In "The Passing of Arthur," he wrote of

"The winter moon,/Brightening the skirts of a long cloud." Elsewhere in Tennyson, an aged man was so old that "a hundred winters snowed upon his breast." So, before we get too flaky, let me snow you.

Névé: First Snow Word

Nowadays *névé* (English borrowed from French) means an area of accumulated older compressed snow or compacted firn above or at the head of a glacier. Perennial névé often blankets high basins or cirques.

Cirque is a technical term in glaciology, also borrowed into English directly from French. Cirque means "a deep steep-walled basin high on a mountain usually shaped like half a bowl and often containing a small lake, caused especially by glacial erosion, and usually forming the blunt head of a valley," so states *Webster's Third New International Dictionary*.

SNOWY TIMELINE

Forty thousand years ago, the word *snow* began as a Proto-Indo-European root with two reflexes, one *nigwh- without initial /s/ and another *snigwh- with /s/. Latin languages (Latin nix, French neige) used the *nigwh- root. Teutonic, Scandinavian, and Slavic tongues adopted the *snigwh root (English *snow*, German *Schnee*, Swedish *snö*, Russian *sneg'*).

But the history of the word *névé* and its protean historical forms are as fascinating to me as what the word itself denotes. In the

French-speaking areas of the Alps, *névé* (orginal meaning "snow") is a direct descendant of the Latin word for snow: *nix, nivis*. Alpine French took the Latin stem *nivis* directly and dropped the Latin declensional genitive /s/ to get *nivi. Then both Latin vowels were extended from i-sounds to e-acute sounds to give the modern reflex, *névé*.

Névé is a form that underwent far less transformation than the standard French word for snow, *neige*, which is also derived from the Latin word *nix, nivis*, in a complex, serial metamorphosis of pronunciatory alterations.

100 B.C.E.: Classical Latin *nix, nivis*
C.E. 1080: Old French *neif, noif*
C.E. 1171: Old French *neu*
Catalan *neu*
Spanish *nieve*
Italian *neve*
Romanian *nea*
Russian *sneg'*
C.E. 1350: Old Northern French *nive*

C.E. 1300–1400—In this century, perhaps, French speakers felt a need to differentiate the pronunciation of their word for snow from their words for nut: *noix* and *noiz*. *Noix* and *nive* began to suffer what is called in linguistics homophonic collision. Both words were used in a very similar manner in that era. Spoken context usually provided the correct meaning of the similar sounding words, but, often enough, French speakers had to add semantic identifier tags such as *neev (I mean the kind that grow on trees). After too many qualifying addendal phrases are added to a word, speakers solve the bother in several ways. A common solution is to alter the pronunciation of one of the troublesomely similar-sounding terms. French linguists posit that *nive* was deliberately elongated to *neige* to unscramble this similarity of pronunciation, but this change had a bit of historical, phonological help too.

C.E. 1431–1485: French poet Francois Villon wrote his most popular ballad *"Des dames du temps jadis"* with its equally famous refrain, *"Mais où sont les neiges d'antan?"* 'But where are the snows of yesteryear?'

How Did It Befall That French *Nive* Became *Neige*?

The altering of *nive* to *neige* was also influenced by a frequentative variant of the common snow verb in various medieval Romance languages. The standard snow verb was: *nevar* in Portuguese, Catalan, and Spanish; *nevre* in Provençal; *never* in Gallo-Roman—all derived from the Late Latin verb *nevere* and its classical Latin ancestor *nivare*.

In Late Latin a frequentative form of the snow verb arose, *nivicare*. At first *nivicare* meant "to snow frequently, to snow for a long time." As so often happened in the history of Romance frequentative verbs, through time a generalization of meaning arose. *Nivicare* and its other forms such as *nevigare* (soft g) came to mean simply "to snow," and then the v-sound disappeared because it was so lightly spoken.

The Final *Neige* Result

The stem of *nivare*, namely *nivic*- could be transformed in some dialectic pronunciations from * "nivitch-" to "nividge-" to the soft-g sound forms "nivige-" to *"neige."* *Et voilà!* Whatever the cause, snow began to be spelled and pronounced *naige* (C.E. 1329), and then *neige* (C.E. 1461).

The dates beside all these words merely indicate their first appearance in French print, either in handwritten manuscripts or printed matter that has survived. They do not tell us when, precisely, French speakers first used such forms. Often spoken words began hundreds of years before they made it into print or into any written record.

Freeze Your Corpse Off

Cryosphere? In a government plan for new studies of Alaska, a recent report spoke of the atmosphere, the lithosphere, the hydrosphere, and the cryosphere. The cryosphere comprises the snow, glaciers, ice caps, as well as lake, river, and sea ice found in a region. Cryosphere is a modern scientific word made up of cryo- from *kryos* Greek "frost, icy cold" + *sphaira* Greek "ball."

Sphaira was borrowed from Koine Greek into an early Late Latin form as *sphera* or *sphæra*, and then into Old French *esphere/espere*. It appeared in English in the thirteenth century. At first in English the word *sphere* referred to the globe of space enclosing the earth and the "ball" of the planet as well. Nowadays, sphere often denotes a specific component of the earth in words such as lithosphere from *lithos* Greek "rock." The lithosphere is the outer part of the earth, made of rock. The hydrosphere is the watery portion of earth and the atmosphere is our vaporous surround of air and gases.

Cryo- Now a Prolific Combining Form

Cryobiology examines components of living things and their function at colder temperatures than their normal.

Cryosurgery, as the distinguishing part of its medical armamentarium, employs surgical instruments that work by applying deep cold to a body part.

Cryonics is a dubious commercial enterprise that deep-freezes dead bodies in the hopes of being able to bring them back to life at a later date. For example, if a deceased person expired of a presently incurable disease, then perhaps in the future the person can be revivified and cured.

Among the scientific drawbacks to this dampish second coming, facilitated by what the freezer boys term "cryonic suspension," is the fact that, when a flash-frozen corpse is unfrozen, almost every cell membrane in the cadaverous body is ruptured, having been partially destroyed during the freezing process itself. Thus, when Uncle Ned is warmly awoken from his frosted sleep, Ned is not going to sit up pertly and begin singing "Take Me Out to the Ball Game." The cryogenically preserved Ned is much more likely to melt into a distressing protoplasmic Slushie that will alarm the children, frighten the household pets, and, should you place him on the verandah for extended family viewing, bring down property values like you wouldn't believe.

Among the notables presently reposing in the gelid bliss of the snowbird seat are Walt Disney and baseball player Ted Williams' severed head.

We'll conclude today's modest cryological excursus with this plaintive quotation from a sports writer's report just after the death of Ted Williams: "What would Ted Williams have thought if he knew his body would be hanging upside down in a nitrogen-filled tank with perhaps four other full bodies and five heads at a cryogenics lab inside a strip mall in Scottsdale, Arizona?"

One cryogenic suspension unit from the Alcor Corporation is the Bigfoot Dewar, which, in the words of the company's promotional literature, is "custom-designed to contain four wholebody patients and six neuropatients immersed in liquid nitrogen at -196 degrees Celsius. The Dewar is an insulated container which consumes no electric power. Liquid nitrogen is added periodically to replace the small amount that evaporates."

One can only paraphrase the famous Goya engraving of 1799, and state that the sleep of reason produces your dead granny as a Corpsicle.

Is It Crap or Is It Kitsch?

I once saw an acrylic painting depicting Jesus in a Modern American beauty salon. It was titled "Christ Gets His Nails Done." It showed the crucifixion nails still in the hands of Jesus being painted by the beautician with purple glitter nail polish. Does that painting desecrate all that is holy and do it in the worst taste possible? I cannot say. To help one make up one's mind, I would remind deciders of a sentence by George Bernard Shaw. He said that every time a savage becomes a Christian, Christianity becomes a little more savage. Shaw's statement proved a trifle too deep for the cross-clutchers, but that diminishes not one whit its veracity. Shaw had a mind that could picnic on a razor blade. It may assist if we define the word *kitsch*, and then seek its origin as a word.

Defining Kitsch

Kitsch is a tricky word to define with precision. In loose, slangy parlance, kitsch is merely "bad art." Wow, that really helps. Who decides what is bad art? Better definitions of kitsch include attention paid to the purpose of the object. Is it trash parading under a flag of high artistic purpose? Then raise the kitsch warning flag too. Does it claim aesthetic purpose, only to prove upon close examination that the object is cheap and tasteless? What about an inflatable, life-size, Mona Lisa, Japanese sex doll with adjustable breasts and "multi-depth" vagina? Yes, it exists. Kitschy-kitschy-koo?

Is it sleazy, mass-produced sentimental crap, such as the Jesus lamp I once saw being offered for sale one block from the Vatican in Rome? When one switched on the lamp, the plaster Jesus figure revolved slowly through 360 degrees and, upon each revolution, Jesus' right arm moved to make the sign of the cross and bless the entire room. Two tiny LEDs, one inside each of Jesus' eyeballs, lit up each time he lamp-blessed the room. For, yea, he is a lamp unto my crossword puzzle. All that was needed was for Jesus to sing, "You Light up My Life." If not kitsch, what utter tat it was!

Bad definitions exist too. For example, the *Oxford English Dictionary* puts far too tight a choke hold on the semantic neck of the word. Opines the lordly OED: kitsch is "art or objets d'art characterized by worthless pretentiousness; the qualities associated with such art or artifacts."

Cleverer by far than the OED's bollocksed statement of meaning is this one by Clement Greenberg in the *Partisan Review* (1939: Rev. VI. 40): "Kitsch is mechanical and operates by formulas. Kitsch is vicarious experience and faked sensations. Kitsch changes according to style, but remains always the same."

Once upon a pleasant 1970s autumn afternoon, in the Toronto kitchen of painter, poet, and art critic Gary Michael Dault, I took part in a discussion about kitsch with Gary's dear friend, Canadian painter Harold Town, one of the most adept draftsmen Canada ever produced. Town insisted that a definition of kitsch centered on the purpose of the art under judgment. Kitsch, said Town, is the product of a creative gesture that only imitates the superficial appearances of art, by repeating clichés and formulae. The purpose of kitsch to reproduce the "look" of original art without any originality brought to bear upon the process, but only copying. In print, Harold Town had earlier stated, "art has no middle ground. Either it works or it doesn't. Bad art is not the enemy; mediocre art is the enemy. Ironically, the impetus for great art seems to grow from the chasm between failure and aspiration . . . ." Kitsch happens when there is no contest between failure and aspiration.

Clement Greenberg and Kitsch

The word *kitsch* became a buzz word during the 1870s among German art critics and later appeared in English print early in the twentieth century. It drifted into English during the next fifty years and flourished in American art criticism from the 1920s onward.

American art critic Clement Greenberg defined it famously in "Avant-Garde and Kitsch," a widely reprinted *Partisan Review* essay as ersatz culture, "for those who, insensible to the values of genuine culture, are hungry nevertheless for the diversion that only culture of some sort can provide." Kitsch can be deceptive, he warned, adding, "It has many different levels, and some of them are high enough to be dangerous to the naïve seeker of true light."

The spread in academic discourse of the word *kitsch* can be traced directly to Greenberg's accurate prophecy. Greenberg had sensitive antennae, finely tuned to pick up alterations in the artistic Zeitgeist. He early recognized that, in the twentieth century, high art (e.g., Mondrian's experiments in space and color) and mass art (the labels on food, plastic toys, advertisements) were distinct but—the wily prediction—destined to influence each other profoundly: all this he said thirty years before Andy Warhol's famous paintings of soup cans appeared. A relative of mine, who shall remain nameless, bought hideous black plastic dish-cleaning gloves, each glove bearing an enormous pink plastic peony flower. Did the flower interfere with the gloves' cleaning efficiency? Of course. Form diminishes function. The gloves are therefore kitschy.

Mass art is trashy but has vulgar élan. One thinks of Noel Coward's remark about "the potency of cheap music." The artist can make the art objects he creates partake of this kitschy street energy by borrowing it. The artist picks up a used egg carton, sprays it orange, and glues it to his latest construction, which also contains a plastic birdcage, a Dinky toy, a doorbell that does not ring, and a whalebone corset with most of the stays missing. Kitsch is sometimes defined by this separation of form from original function. The egg carton has its dull, daily usefulness as an object that holds and protects eggs, and then is tossed into the paper-recycling bin. But now, glued to an artwork, the piece as kitsch gives off new visual and semantic vibrations as part of a campy construction. "It's good because it's awful," wrote Susan Sontag in "Notes on 'Camp' " in her book *Against Interpretation*. We admit the garish or sentimental crappiness of the original object; at the same time we enjoy its very kitschiness.

In less formal criticism of popular art, kitsch is still used in its original German sense to mean "low-brow junk of poor quality," for example, "That painting of Elvis as a bullfighter on black velvet fighting off an army of charging pills is pure kitsch."

Etymology of the Word *Kitsch*

The origin is unclear. Three or four origins are suggested. The etymology I find most cogent claims that the word *kitsch* was borrowed from German *Rotwelsch* "thieves' slang" some time in the 1870s. In the cant of German crooks, *kitschen* was a verb that meant "to pull the old switcheroo on a mark." A dishonest antique dealer places in his shop window a genuine antique candlestick. When a naïve customer enters to buy it, the dealer shows the trusting customer the genuine article. The customer agrees to buy the candlestick. The dealer takes it to the back of the shop *und er ist gekitscht!* "He is tricked with a switch!" The dealer substitutes a fake candlestick and keeps the original antique to sell to the next innocent who happens into the shop. German art critics borrowed the verb, made it a noun, and applied it to phoney art that only looked like real art, but was in fact spurious.

Now, *kitschen* earlier meant "to scrape up mud from the street" and hence "to put something together in a slapdash manner." That, too, could be an influencing semantic hue on the eventual meaning of kitsch in art.

Another possible source, although it is later than the crooks' cant, may be the German verb *verkitschen etwas*, "to make a knock-off, to manufacture a cheap imitiation of." One German verb meaning "to cheapen" is *verkitschen*. *Verkitschen* also has a slang meaning "to flog shoddy goods."

Artists Considered Kitschy

Norman Rockwell (American 1894–1978) was branded as American kitsch once upon a time, as were the pseudo-pornographic nudes of the Frenchman William-Adolphe Bouguereau (1825–1905), the American illustrations of Maxfield Parrish (1870–1966), and the treacly work of Thomas Kinkade (American, 1958–), whose spuming oceans and twee cottages with twinkling candles in the windows have been called "utter kitsch." But taste changes as time flows. None of the kitsch labels has prevented some of their paintings from fetching hundreds of thousands of dollars at art auctions.

The Birth of Venus

The kitsch classic may be "The Birth of Venus" painted in 1879 by a popular and rich French artist of the day, William-Adolphe Bouguereau. This florid fountain of toddler flesh, bustling with implicit pedophilia and adult pre-copulative entwinement, starring a porno Venus at its centre, is a classic of something. In the painting, Venus' yummy pudendum is all shaved and pumiced, so that timorous, boyish males viewing her will not be put off by the depiction of a mature and powerful female body with pubic and axillary hair that announces sexual allure and feminine potency. Such a depilatory fastidiousness almost always betokens pornography.

During France's nineteenth-century fin-de-siècle, oceans of succulent pink flesh were perfectly fit for the nouveau-bourgeois Parisian parlor, so long as their pornographic subtext was disguised and filtered by a tasteful reference to classical mythology. After all, those ancient Greeks were pretty much a bunch of Boy Scouts, weren't they? The proliferation of merit badges in Attic buggery was a mere coincidence of the era, right?

In "The Birth of Venus" form overpowers function, if we agree that the purpose of the painting is to depict a mythic event. But— all that criticism said—some viewers of this painting consider it "high art," stating that it delivers an aesthetic frisson which entitles it to the label "masterpiece."

In conclusion, I must let loose the etymologist in me. This birth of Venus depicts the goddess of love rising from a seashell. The ancient Romans borrowed that origin story from Greek mythology, where it resides in the very name of the Greek goddess of love, their equivalent of Venus, namely, Aphrodite. *Aphros* means "sea foam" and *ditos* "sprung from." A goddess named Aphrodite rising from a seashell is a simple sexual graphic reference. The sea foam is sperm and the seashell cloven open is the birth gate of the vagina. Here the sexual necessaries of human reproduction are pleasantly symbolized and civilly presented—to ancient viewers who knew what they were looking at and did not blush. Instead they smiled, recognizing art as opposed to kitsch.

Conclusion

A living language is just that. English is alive; English is organic; English changes daily, weekly, yearly. Spoken and written words are like living tissue. We use them and the sandpaper of time abrades them. Scuffed and grated by a million mouths, words wither away, through overuse or change of meaning; then each language sloughs old words off, the same way that living tissue casts off old cells to make way for new growth.

Sometimes the spelling of a word gives us a peek at its original meaning. Awful once meant "reverent, full of awe"; now it means "of bad quality." Other words have been transformed so thoroughly that we can no longer see their original meanings without etymological poking. Every person who discusses words, teaches languages, or deals with the public on linguistic matters, finds it exceedingly difficult to convince the general public that change is a natural, inevitable function of English. When people who have not studied and thought about language hear the speech around them altering, hear new slang words assaulting their well-bred ears, they tend to freak. Then they dash off letters to the editor, fretful that words they love are disappearing or gaining new meanings. That can't be proper, they whine. The severe short forms of digital texting frighten some older people into thinking we have entered a new Dark Age of illiteracy at the letterless conclusion of which shambling monosyllabic grunts will have replaced the sweet flow of crisp English. Don't worry. It ain't gonna happen. Promise!

Our language exists in history; English moves through time, and, as English-speakers tiptoe through the floribundant and verbiferous meadows of temporality, meeting new influences, bringing back from strange shores new foreign words, our vocabulary expands. Sometimes brash upstarts coin new words. I just coined floribundant meaning "abounding in flowers" because I thought it sounded pleasant in the first sentence of this paragraph. So sue me.

With English, change is the only constant. In semantics we can quote the Greek philosopher Heraclitus whose core belief he stated as *"panta rei"* Greek for "all things flow." You can't step in the same stream of meaning twice. So, no more letters to the *New York Times* about the decline of the semicolon in the works of Dr. Seuss. Okey-dokey? In language, change is here to stay.

Index

A

Aasvogel, 37

Ablaut, 127–28

Adobe Wells (TX), 7–8

Affinage, 109

Ahoy, 61

Alambique Creek (CA), 9

Alameda (CA), 12

Alamillo and Alamocita (NM), 12

Alamo (TX), 10–11

Alamogordo (NM), 12

Albatross, 8–9

Alcatraz (CA), 8–9

Alembic, 9

Algonquian words, 14, 15–16, 17

Alias, 45

Alibi, 45

Alien, and word relatives, 43–45

Alkali Lake or Alkali Flats, 10

Allegheny River, 13–14

Alluvion, 75–77

Al- places, 9

Ambimextrous, 140–41

American place names, 5–18. *See also specific names*

    Arabic words hidden in, 6–10

    cottonwood-related, 11–12

    Hic sunt dracones ('here be dragons') and, 6

    Native American river names, 13–18

    polis words, 201

    Spanish (Latin) origins, 10–13

    toponyms and, 6

Animal oddities, 33–39. *See also specific animals*

Anima words, 13

Annapolis (MD), 201

Annatto, 109

Apocope, 145

Arabic words

    apple, for smiling, 107

    hidden in American place names, 6–10

    for pepper, 91–92

Argosy, 63–64

Arrowhead tubers, 17

Assimilation, 222

Asterisk (*) in front of word, 23

Atmos words, 13

Augury/augur, 211–13, 214–17

Auspex, 213–14

Avast, 61

Avulsion, 77

Axolotl, 37–38

About the Author

Bill Casselman is one of Canada's leading etymologists. He spent twenty-two years as a writer, director, and producer for CBC Radio and CBC TV, the Canadian equivalents of NPR and PBS in the U.S.A. He has published ten books on the origins of Canadian words and sayings, three of them bestsellers—one of them stayed in the Canadian Top Ten in Canada's *National Post* newspaper book pages for sixty-three weeks. He is also the author of a medical dictionary and numerous magazine and newspaper columns and articles. He is a columnist at *Vocabula*, the leading American online word magazine. You may contact him at *canadiansayings@mountaincable.net* and visit his website at *www.billcasselman.com*.

DAILY BENDER

Want Some More?

Hit up our humor blog, The Daily Bender, to get your fill of all things funny—be it subversive, odd, offbeat, or just plain mean. The Bender editors are there to get you through the day and on your way to happy hour. Whether we're linking to the latest video that made us laugh or calling out (or bullshit on) whatever's happening, we've got what you need for a good laugh.

If you like our book, you'll love our blog. (And if you hated it, man up and tell us why.) Visit The Daily Bender for a shot of humor that'll serve you until the bartender can.

VISIT THE DAILY BENDER BLOG TODAY AT
www.adamsmedia.com/blog/humor